FRESHWATER GAME FISH
OF NORTH AMERICA
SILVIO CALABI

FRESHWATER GAME FISH
OF NORTH AMERICA
SILVIO CALABI

THE WELLFLEET PRESS

Editorial Director: Frank Oppel
Design Director: Tony Meisel
Origination by Regent Publishing Services, Ltd.
Printed by Leefung-Asco Printers, Ltd.

Manufactured in Hong Kong.

ISBN: 1-55521-520-3

Contents

Introduction 7

Bass 9

Catfish 27

Grayling 34

Panfish 36

Perch 46

Pikes 50

Sea-Run Fish 68

Shad 94

Sheefish 96

Trout 98

World Records 135

Index 141

Introduction

IT WAS IN POSTWAR EUROPE that I arrived on the fishing scene—hardly more than a toddler, strapped securely into a kiddie seat on the back of my uncle's bicycle. Lashed to the bike behind me was always a live bucket, a copper-colored thing with a hinged top and air holes, which was empty when we set out to go fishing but that must have been hell's own headache for my uncle to pedal back home when it was full of water and fish. Especially with a cane pole clamped to each handlebar in his fingers and a three-year-old nephew riding caboose.

This was Switzerland, where no road stays on the level for long.

We'd wobble down the lane and around a few bends to where a wooden bridge spanned a minor stream, and there we'd dismount. My uncle filled the live well and set it in the nearshore current, so water would bubble through the holes, and then we'd get down to business. He kept a small hunk of cheese at the bridge, out of sight on a beam, for bait; I had to lie on my stomach next to one of the railing uprights and reach down and under for it. Wonderfully scary. It wasn't the Swiss cheese we know, for it could be rolled into sticky balls and plastered onto the hooks. We lowered our armament into the quiet eddies behind rocks, then laid the poles flat in the gaps between the bridge floorboards and lay down ourselves as well, so we could peer down into that strange world through cupped hands.

Small fish materialized immediately. I can still see them, I think, hovering in quarrelsome bunches of three or five around each bait until the hungriest or the most foolish or the biggest or the littlest, overcome by the need to get it before its rivals did, screwed up its courage and rushed forward into oblivion. I don't remember what they were—a few were not trout certainly, for I do recall my uncle showing me a certain way to hold a fish, not more than six or eight inches long, so its stiff dorsal spines wouldn't harm me. Perch?

Each one went into the live bucket, then home and into the bathtub, of all things. My entrepreneurial uncle didn't have a paper route; he had a fish route. I remember only one of his accounts, the local parish priest, because of the dark and gloomy rectory we delivered our catch to. Vaguely, and finally, I remember a couple of domestic scenes involving our fish gasping on the floor in the bathroom, large puddles of water, and my grandmother, perhaps with hands on her hips .

The memory of this beginning has come to me twice most strongly: Once on my first visit—an adult now, or as close as I'll come—to Yellowstone Park, when I hung over Fishing Bridge with hundreds of other rubber-neckers to watch the opportunistic cutthroat trout snap up cigarette butts seemingly an arm's length away; and again a couple of years ago, as I waited for a floatplane on the dock of a lodge in the western Alaskan bush. I was sitting on a duffle, idly peering through the spaces between the boards into the clear river below. That and something else—could it have been a whiff of cheese from the lodge kitchen?—triggered a rush of *déjà vu* that almost spilled me over. It had the force of a sudden wave of tropical fever.

Maybe you can see that my life has become involved with fishing to an extent that no one could have guessed on that canton bridge. At every turn of my working life, when I made the choices that have led me here, the route seemed obvious; the path of least resistance. And at every new development in my "career," when others congratulated me or commented on my "job," I was able to keep a straight face and mumble something appropriate, while thinking gleefully, *"Sure beats working!"*

I can think of no other more common denominator for humankind—except maybe food or sex—than this fascination with peering into water to see what gives with the fish. Almost 32 million fishing licenses were sold in the U.S.A. last year, and that doesn't count the kids and saltwater fishermen who didn't need licenses. Sophisticated Swedish bankers do it. Mighty Japanese industrialists lose their cool completely over foot-long trout. A Bhutanese Buddhist monk, immersed in a centuries-old reverence for life, will struggle with his conscience only briefly before sidling over next to a Western angler to see how they're bitin'. Eskimos, Southern Baptists, Chinese peasants, Soviet apparatchiks and Wall Street traders all drop what they're doing at the chance to mess around with fish.

Analysts say they—we—are all transferring, seeking to trade places with wild, free things, to reduce our cares to their least state and restore harmony to our lives. Yes, certainly. And I say we all have some ancient memory of a bridge, or a farm pond, or a jetty, and the things that swam through the water to touch us.

Silvio Calabi
Camden, Maine

Bass

THE LARGE-MOUTHED BLACK BASS. (MICROPTERUS SALMOIDES.)

THE LARGEMOUTH BASS has spawned, ahem, an industry. In fact the large-mouth bass has *become* an industry. If there are truly sixty million sportfish-ermen in America, as estimated, then probably forty of those millions regard this largest of the sunfish family as nu-mero uno on the hit parade. Bass fishing has become a sport unto itself, like trout fishing, but it's even more closely de-fined: For starters, there is only one largemouth bass (there are lots of differ-ent trout). And to "bass-fish" in the fullest sense one needs a large stable of advanced-composite-materials bassin' rods, each carrying an extraordinarily high-tech reel (with readouts for lure depth and speed); a kitchen-appliance-size tackle box of bass lures designed to swim, kick, pop, twist, gurgle and emit sexy scents at every level of the water column; an array of electronic water depth, temperature, pH and turbidity meters that would make a Soviet sub commander jealous; a bass boat (the performance of which is the envy of *any* navy and most drug runners) on which to stow all this gear, as well as food, beer, CB radio, stereo sound and the bass you do catch; a bass trailer; a bass four-wheel-drive; and a collection of jaunty bass caps and one-piece bass jumpsuits. The bass Winnebago is optional, as are the "kiss my bass" T-shirts and panties for your girlfriend. And then after you've learned to put this gear to the proper use, you may consider joining the bass tournament

9

A smallmouth bass warily holding its ground above the "structure" it calls home. Gilbert van Ryckevorsel photograph.

circuit, where the cash prizes are second only to pro golf and tennis.

The most interesting thing is that the largemouth just happens to be worth all this.

It possesses all the hallmarks of a great gamefish: a voracious appetite that regards everything from ducklings to its own offspring as table fare; a no-nonsense approach to feeding that often leaves the successful fisherman with cardiac palpitations; impressive strength and size; and a combination of low cunning and high intelligence that has proven the bass to be the smartest of our fish. Furthermore, thanks to stocking, largemouth bass are now found in every state, in all of Mexico and Central America, and throughout much of Canada and Europe.

Bass are warmwater fish. Although they thrive in the cool lakes of Michigan, Maine, Oregon and so on, they positively thrive in the warm, fecund waters of, say, Texas and Florida. Where there's lots of food year-round and where the more jungly landscape provides the kind of subsurface cover bass like to skulk around in. One of the bass fisherman's biggest challenges is to present his lures without hanging up on lily pads, water grasses, or drowned trees and brush. The next challenge is to provoke one of those heart-stopping strikes. Tests show the largemouth learns faster than other fish, and so grows jaded by baits and artificial lures. Once the fish recognizes everything you've got, sometimes the only solution is to find a new lure the fish hasn't yet seen. (Hence the van-sized tackle boxes.)

But you don't really need all the aforementioned materiel just to catch *a* bass (*the* bass, the local monster, perhaps so). Largemouth bass can be taken on all sorts of tackle, even streamer flies and flyrod poppers, and from canoes, float tubes and even from shore. It's just that catching one big, head-shaking, gill-rattling, bulldogging bass naturally makes you want to catch another, and another, and a bigger one. . . . Down that road lies the perfectly understandable bass madness that keeps tackle makers in business.

The largemouth bass, America's most popular gamefish. Minnesota Dept. of Natural Resources photograph.

An illustration of why the largemouth bass is familiarly known as both "bucketmouth" and "hawg"—and why it is such a popular gamefish. Scientific Anglers/3M photograph.

A rock bass investigates a bait while bluegill sunfish wait. Photograph by Doug Stamm.

A fly-caught smallmouth bass from Lake Memphremagog, on the Vermont-Quebec border. Photograph by Jerry Gibbs.

Small 'silver," or white, bass, photographed by Don Blegen.

A largemouth bass that took one of the most successful lures of all time, a rubber worm. Scientific Anglers/3M photograph.

A rock bass lunging after a streamer fly. Photograph by Doug Stamm.

A largemouth bass striking a lure. Scientific Anglers/3M photograph.

Smallmouth bass attacking a spinner lure. Photograph by Doug Stamm.

A cruising largemouth bass changes course to inspect the fisherman's bogus worm. Scientific Anglers/3M photograph.

The **smallmouth bass** is almost as popular, but maybe with a slightly different breed of angler— these fish live in deeper or cooler water, and often in rivers that may also be trout habitat. Smallmouths are smaller than largemouth bass (although the official world record of twelve-plus pounds would be respectable for a bigmouth too), a bit more streamlined, as befits fish that live in moving water, and often show indistinct dark vertical bars on their bronze-brown hide. The smallmouth naturally has a smaller mouth, too— the point of its jaw does not extend back past the eye, as on its larger cousin— so it isn't capable of swallowing the sort of prey that largemouth have built their reputation upon. But the smallmouth is a heavy feeder nonetheless, an ambusher of live food, and just as gamy an adversary on rod & line.

The scientists who proclaim the largemouth the smartest of our gamefish also rank the smallmouth highly. Only devoted smallmouth anglers disagree— they say their fish is much harder to fool consistently.

In a shallow, clear stream, you can sight-fish to a pair of these bass for a whole afternoon without a) spooking them or b) catching one. But that's no reason not to try: Start right at the tail of a pool, where the constricted flow and greater current concentrate the food passing by. If a baitfish lure doesn't bring a strike, consider switching to fly tackle and seductively twitching a feathery leech pattern through the same water, down near the bottom. Failing that, a couple of box-stock trout flies, such as a little nymph or even a generic dry fly, may bring a strike. If the fish have seen all this before, it may be time for the closest thing to a sure-fire smallmouth "gitter"— live bait, in the form of a crayfish lightly hooked through the tail. Your target fish may fall upon this offering with the equivalent of glad cries, interrupting only to bash each other away from your hook. It's almost sad to see such smart alecks turn instantly into gibbering idiots.

After these two black basses, the handsome **crappie**— pronounced "croppie"— is the next largest of the sunfish (probably in popularity as well as in size). Crappies come in black and white varieties— the former often preferring cooler, deeper, sometimes moving water, the latter more a southern shallows-dweller, but there is plenty of crossover.

Crappie grow sometimes as large as four pounds, with the distinctive pear-shaped bodies of "sunnies." Their most unusual feature is their fins: Both anal and dorsal fins are very similar in size and shape (like long, graceful Japanese fans) and are located almost directly one above the other, just aft of the midline of the body. Few freshwater fish show such bilateral symmetry, so crappies are easy to identify in general. It's telling the black from the white that's harder, as they are commonly the same color— dark green/olive/black backs above silvery sides. And both are heavily spotted. But the spots on the white crappie are arranged more or less into irregular vertical bars, while the black crappie's spots are sprinkled on haphazardly. And scientists say the black crappie has seven or eight spines in its dorsal fin while the white has no more than six.

Crappies are often uninterested in surface feeding, so the angler should go down to them. These quick-striking fish fall for a great variety of lures— everything from live minnows to small spinners and spoons to flyrod streamers. They congregate in large schools and, like all sunfish, are particularly susceptible in defense of their spring spawning grounds. (You may in fact be reminded of the old saw about shooting fish in a barrel.) Reportedly, when biologist Elgin Ciampi tested eight fish species for intelligence, the crappie scored a lowly seventh— ahead of only the gar— in learning to avoid lures. Once you've located a school, the most difficult aspect of boating crappies may be hanging onto them— their mouth tissue is very fragile and hooks tear out easily. But if you use a net you'll soon be in good shape for a fish fry.

A predatory largemouth accelerates forward to inhale a small sunfish, which is stiffening its dorsal spines in a vain attempt to discourage the attack. Scientific Anglers/3M photograph.

THE SMALL-MOUTHED BLACK BASS. (Micropterus dolomieu.)

Catfish

THE BULLHEAD
(AMIURUS NEBULOSUS)

THE SERIOUS CATFISHERMAN is a breed apart, something of a rarity among us sporting types. The catfish, in all its species, is different too, at least among the fish in this book; it is a bottom feeder. The catfish's appearance is unique also, among gamefish: snaky barbels, which are in fact sensitive organs of touch/ smell that let the fish prosper in low visibility, sprout from its mouth and chin like the mustachios of a comic-book villain. The mouth is flat and wide, like a rubbery gash across its flat and even wider shovel-shaped head. The eyes appear piggy and small. Its slaty gray-brown or blue-black hide bears no scales at all, and reflects little light. None of the coruscating beauty of a brook trout here. This is obviously a creature of the deep, and men who would have it must go there in pursuit; the catfish won't be lured upward.

There are two reasons for wanting to do this. First, inevitably, the challenge: A big catfish— some get *very* big— is a tough customer. And second, catfish, and their close relatives the hornpout, are superb table fare, so much so that they have

been a major aquacultural crop in the South for decades. Despite their looks, catfish are not garbage feeders, and your first taste of catfish fry will confirm this— like us, catfish are what they eat, and they are delicious.

But back to the challenge. The big-water **blue catfish** is the largest prize. Specimens approaching 120 pounds have been hoisted (on very heavy gear) from deep, swift Mississippi River tailwaters, and 200-pounders were reportedly taken in Civil War times. In the right places today, thirty-pounders are almost everyday catches. Blues can be awesome predators, feeding on other fish and crayfish, and are usually caught on natural baits that would astonish most freshwater fishermen— whole large suckers, for instance. **Channel catfish** also like deep water and clean bottoms, in larger rivers and lakes. Channel cats have deeply forked tails, are often spotted, and are maybe "sportier" than blues— they will often strike artificial lures like deep-running spoons. Although they grow to fifty pounds or so, five- to ten-pound channel cats are

27

impressive gamefish. They too are voracious predators and, with generally sleeker bodies than other catfish, fast swimmers that sometimes enter small streams to spawn.

(They seem to tolerate colder water too: Around 1980, a boy fishing for trout hooked and landed what proved to be a tremendous channel cat—in a Vermont stream. The uproar among local fly fishermen was spectacular, but eventually died down when it became clear that the trout were not being decimated and that there were no more big cats. One theory is that the fish was planted, as a prank, by someone visiting the area in a motorhome.)

The olive-drab **flathead** is the third of North America's giant catfish, and it too is most plentiful in the Mississippi corridor. It's easy to distinguish because it is the only cat with a rounded, blunt tail, like a hornpout's, while its size and distinctively disagreeable looks (it is appropriately named) set it well apart from the 'pouts too. A big one goes about a hundred pounds and maybe sixteen inches between the eyes, but ten pounds is normal. Flatheads—sometimes known as mudcats—are pure predators, and they can be found in shallow water,

lurking in ambush in their riverbank lairs like pike. Thus the "sport" of noodling for flatheads: A fisherman cautiously wades to the den, eases his arm into the dark water, and ever so slowly feels around until he can suddenly thrust his hand into the fish's gaping mouth, grab a gill, and heave the monster onto the bank. Fun, eh? You might well wonder who caught whom. Tales of noodlers who were themselves dragged kicking and screaming underwater abound in catfish country.

Specialists who go after big cats have many methods to choose from, but if you leave off nets, traps and the like and concentrate on hook & line, the basics involve a huge sinker, to hold the offering on the bottom in heavy current, and, tied into the line above, one or more huge hooks baited with something revolting. As in chicken guts, smelly cheese, oil-soaked sponges, doughballs,

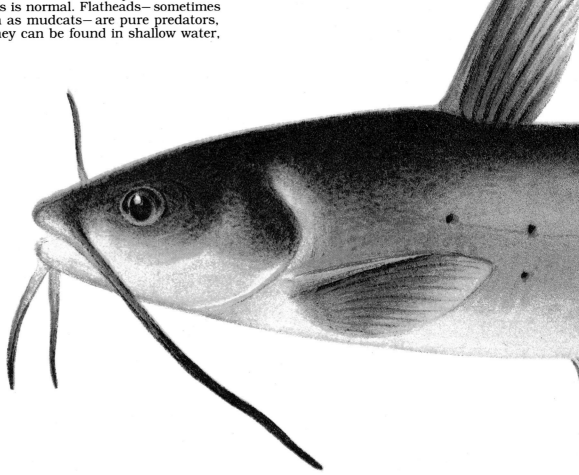

SPOTTED CATFISH (ICTALURUS PUNCT

frogs and whole or sectioned fish. Catfish baits needn't even be edible, at least by human standards; there is a school of catfishermen who rely on different brands of soap for bait. At the other end of the line there's usually some sort of stout float—anything from commercial plastic bobbers to milk jugs. Catfish are nocturnal feeders, and perhaps you can imagine the pandemonium caused by a hookup with a huge fish in the dark, on a heavy flowing, tricky river.

There's one more important American cat, the comparatively small and meek **white catfish** that lives on the East and West coasts and in Great Lakes rivers. The recorded world record is a mere seventeen and a half pounds, and a ten-pounder is rare. But whites are top pan-fish also, and kids from Maine to Michigan to California have learned to catch them on pint-sized versions of the tackle used in the Midwest.

Hornpout—or maybe horned pout, or bullpout, or bullheads—are members of the catfish family distinguished by their small size and rounded tails. One or another of the 'pout species (brown, black, yellow, flathead, etc.) are found in almost every part of America, and annually millions of them find their way into skillets and freezers.

While a big river cat is pounds and

pounds of moist, succulent white meat, a little bullhead, undressed for the pan, is often pinkish, equally tasty, and sized and shaped like an ear of corn. And, after deep-frying, that's just how you eat them.

One of my earliest memories of fishing is watching the neighborhood nannies and cleaning ladies catch hornpout in the evenings, grouped companionably together on folding chairs on the beach of a tiny lake in the town where I grew up. The fish never seemed to die, thrashing in the pails no matter how long the owner stayed at the lake. (When I grew older and could catch them for myself, I discovered that, eerily, they truly never did seem to die, or at least they never stopped squirming, even after being gutted and skinned!)

Hornpout are as important to an American childhood as sunfish. They are easy to catch—just heave out a hook decorated with worms or a bit of leftover school lunch; abundant almost everywhere there are muddy ponds; and ugly and just dangerous enough, thanks to that sharp spine on the fins that can inflict a painful stab, to thrill kids deeply. Now that I think about it, how come more of us don't graduate from bullheads to full emotional involvement with catfish?

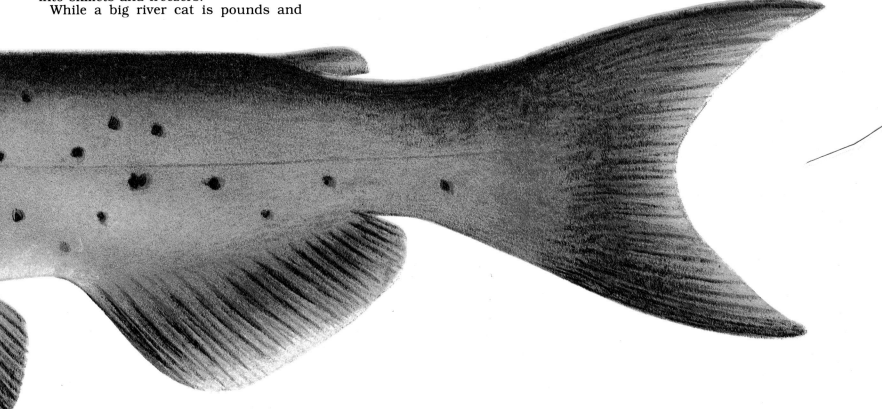

S (RAFINESQUE)]

A tackle-caught channel catfish, showing net marks on its smooth sides and destined for the table. Don Blegen photograph.

A small blue catfish investigates the lake bottom with its sensitive barbels. Minnesota Dept. of Natural Resources photograph.

Grayling

THE GRAYLING is a trickster among North American gamefish. The bigger ones, that hide in deep pools and runs, strike a hook and fight like Dolly Varden or even small salmon. But the little fellows, the ones that pop up in the riffles or in calm, sun-warmed shallows, dimple the surface like panfish. The grayling is a puzzle in other ways too— in unfished wilderness waters they can become stubbornly selective, while at other times it seems a bit of parka lining on a hook will attract a mob. It's a shame more fishermen don't get to see them, but they're a northern fish, found in great numbers only in Alaska and north-western Canada. Remnant populations exist down into the American Rockies, and a century ago they were so populous in the upper Midwest as to be commercial market fish.

In spite of this rarity, everyone knows the grayling— it's that pretty little number with the iridescent purplish-greenish-silvery hide and the huge dorsal fin. It's probably this fancy dress, and the fact that they live in sportfishing country, that elevates grayling to the ranks of great gamefish, for they are not spectacular fighters. (After all, how much tussle can you expect from a fish that tops out at two or three pounds?) Grayling can be caught on flies, lures and bait with equal success. Many Alaskan anglers look to the grayling for rest from the salmon and trout battles; after days of slugging it out with heavy tackle in big water, it can be a welcome change to pick up ultralight tackle and stalk active, surface-feeding two-pound grayling. They are excellent table fare, too; stranded in the Cassiar Mountains of northern British Columbia, four of us ate grayling for two weeks straight and never tired of that firm, delicate white meat.

Interested in an IGFA world record? The streams of the west-central coast of Alaska shelter the biggest grayling I've seen anywhere. I released one of twenty-four inches there in the summer of '86, and plenty only a little smaller.

Its showy dorsal fin distinguishes the arctic grayling. This large specimen was taken in British Columbia by the photographer, David Lambroughton.

Panfish

IT'S AN UGLY WORD, but it's going to stick around, even among the millions of fishermen who prefer *not* to pop them into a skillet at day's end: panfish. The angling equivalent of "small game." Sure, it's hard to strike a heroic pose with a stringer of shellcrackers, just like a beltfull of squirrels isn't quite the same as an eight-point whitetail. But that shouldn't relegate panfish to second-class-fish status. While they are certainly not big-game fish, and you may not regard them as gamefish, no one can dispute that they are game fish, if you see what I mean.

These fish are game as can be, in fact—quick as rattlesnakes to defend their mate and nest, pugnacious fighters on hook & line, strong and handsome and even plentiful. Although the word panfish can be applied to hornpout, yellow perch, crappie and other species, I'm talking about the smaller sunfishes, such as the **bluegill**.

If bluegill grew to the size of, say, Frisbees, no one would pay attention to permit any more; they would simply have been upstaged as one of earth's hardest-fighting fish. The bluegill's broad, flat sides give it tremendous "traction" in the water, and when you back that kind of leverage up with the muscle and disposition of a predator, you have a gutsy opponent that can make your line sing as it cuts doughnuts through the water. But bluegills rarely grow larger than eight or ten inches, and, as they often live cheek-by-gills with largemouth bass, many fall for bass gear that is just too heavy for proper sport.

But arm yourself with wispy tackle and stalk the bluegill and its many cousins on purpose. They'll go for almost anything—tiny spinners and spoons, all manner of cheese, worms and other bait, maybe even a scrap of your T-shirt on a weighted hook. But truly the best way to fish for them is with a fly rod. Not a designer bamboo mounted with an English reel (well, then again, . . .) but a floppy old glass rod and your uncle's hand-me-down automatic, and a handful of rubber-legged, horribly colored little

A happy fisherman with the makings of a crappie bake for the whole neighborhood. He uses the long pole to reach deep into brushy pockets where the fish feel protected. William Greer photograph.

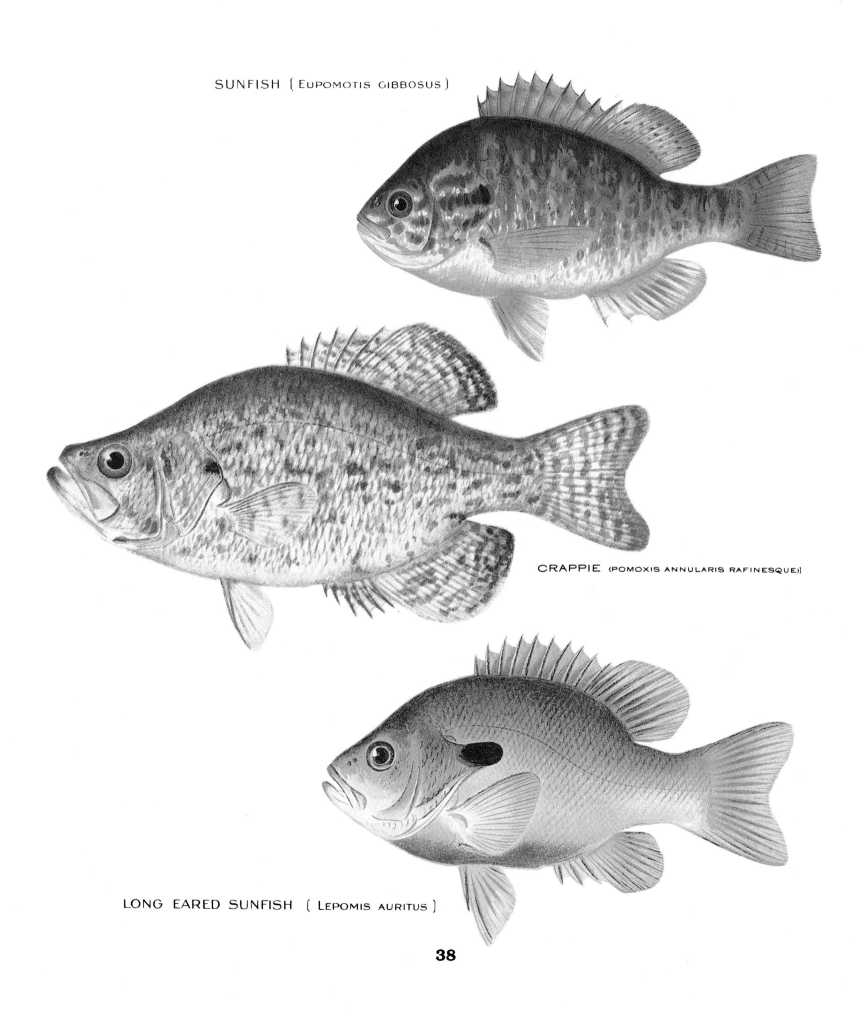

SUNFISH (Eupomotis gibbosus)

CRAPPIE (Pomoxis annularis rafinesque)]

LONG EARED SUNFISH (Lepomis auritus)

38

Bluegill sunfish, photographed by Don Blegen.

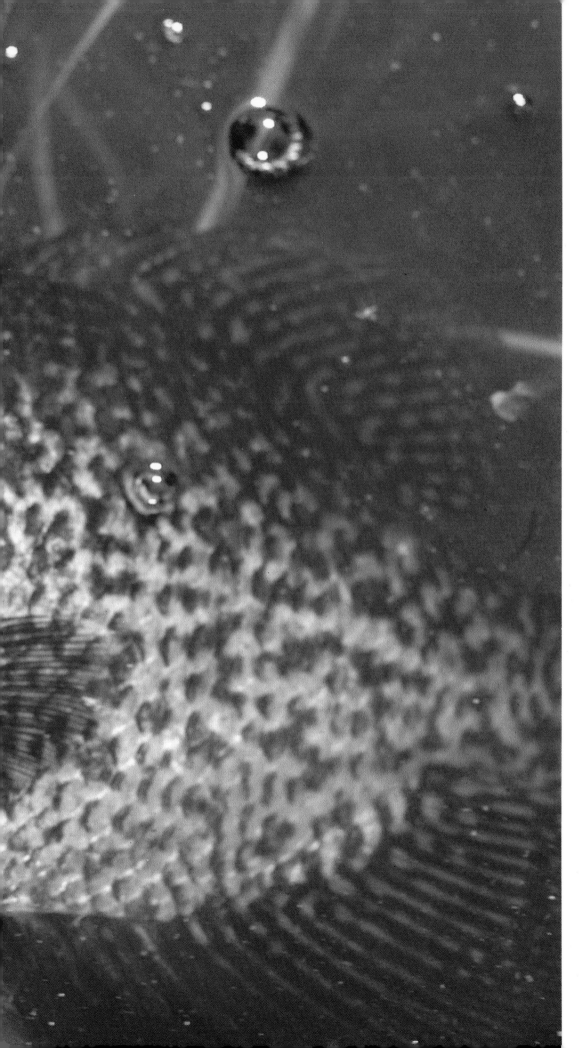

A crappie, the panfisherman's delight.
Photograph by Don Blegen.

topwater poppers. There's no need here for the far-and-fine fly presentation of the trout angler; just plop that thing down in the warm summer shallows near a weed bed and twitch it a bit.

A bluegill strikes a popper with pursed lips that make a distinctive kissing noise as they break the surface. On a still day, in clear water, it's fascinating to watch blugills hover underneath, inspecting the fly, then dart upward to smack it. It's the best way I know to learn to handle fly tackle and have fun at the same time.

Bluegills have, uh, blue gills. That is, the little "ear" flap at the rear of their gill covers is deep blue or even black and lacks the contrasting red-orange spot typical of most sunfish. The **pumpkinseed** has it, but it almost disappears in this fish's brilliant coloring, which runs to green-blue stripes radiating across its orange head and stomach, and olive green back and sides shot through with more orange or yellow. The **red-ear sunfish**, widely known in its native South as the shellcracker, for the teeth with which it grinds up snails, looks much like a toned-down pumpkinseed but has a distinctive red edge to its gill flap and no bands across its head. Red-ears grow to an impressive three pounds-plus, eating almost anything and everything—in some Alabama lakes, for example, they feed heavily at the surface on willowfly hatches, just like trout. There's also a **redbreast** sunfish, which look like it should be a bluegill-pumpkinseed cross but isn't, that lives in East-Coast smallmouth rivers; a **green** sunfish that is almost as streamlined as a bass; the tiny **longear** sunfish, which prefers cooler and often flowing water; **spotted** sunfish; and a host of hybrids that only add to the fishing—and the confusion.

A redbreast sunfish, photographed by Joel Arrington.

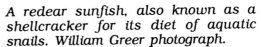

A redear sunfish, also known as a shellcracker for its diet of aquatic snails. William Greer photograph.

A school of bluegill sunfish. Minnesota Dept. of Natural Resources photograph.

Perch

THE PIKE PERCH OR WALL-EYED PIKE (Stizostedium Vitreum)

RIGHT UP THERE alongside the large-mouth bass and the entire trout family in popularity with American fishermen is the homely **walleye**. For a fish to be so well-known and loved, it must be wide-ranging—which it is, occurring naturally and through stocking in Canada and all but the Gulf Coast states—and it must have some outstanding attributes as a gamefish. The walleye is not a water-thrashing, tackle-tearing fighter. Nor is it so beautiful an animal that we seek it out just to photograph it or mount it. But it *is* 1) fairly easy to catch, 2) ugly enough that no one seems to mind knocking it over the head, and 3) very tasty.

The walleye's wide range is why it has so many—dozens, in fact—local names. It's not a pike, despite its teeth and predatory habits; rather it is the largest member of the perch family, with the characteristic second dorsal fin. (The current IGFA record is a twenty-five pounder caught in 1960 in Tennessee.) Anyone who has ever seen a walleye understands the name immediately—its eyes do in fact look helplessly blind and

opaque. The opposite is true, though, particularly at night, when those big eyes become a huge advantage in feeding. Ironically, they help fishermen locate them as well, for they reflect light noticeably, even underwater.

Look for walleyes near the bottom of fairly clean, fairly cool waters—lakes and slower-moving rivers. Many successful fishermen slowly troll baitfish imitations along the drop-offs from shallow to deep water. When the first walleye hits, they anchor to still-fish, for they know that these fish often congregate in large schools.

The walleye's humble relative, the **yellow perch**, is a member of that loose category known as panfish. And appropriately, like the walleye perch, the yellow variety is worth popping into a pan. (Certainly it is on no one's endangered-species list—it's one of the few gamefish that shows up in probably every state.) Its meat is white, delicate and in enough demand that there is a substantial commercial fishery for perch in the Great Lakes.

A netted walleye; note its enlarged eye pupil. Photograph by Doug Stamm.

A walleye entering the net, photographed by Doug Stamm.

The sweatshirt says it all—fisherman's luck. Don Blegen photographed this boy's trophy walleye.

A brightly colored yellow perch that fell victim to a rubber-legged "slider" fly. Joel Arrington photograph.

Like the pike and the striped bass, the yellow perch is one of the most easily recognized fish, thanks to the half-dozen or more vertical dark bars that pepper its yellowish body, and the twin dorsal fins. Perch strike lures, flies and bait pretty much all year round— in fact, they are a popular target of ice-fishermen. While boatloads of us adults secretly get a kick out of perch, I suspect their greatest value is to kids. I know full well that I wouldn't be writing this today if it hadn't been for the hundreds of scrappy little perch that obligingly sunk my bobbers thirty and more years ago.

A bragging-size walleye— not a pike but a perch. Jim Lindner, The In-Fisherman, photograph.

Pikes

The northern pike normally waits in ambush for foodfish, then strikes and withdraws in an eyeblink, its prey often clamped crosswise in its jaws the way a dog carries a bone. Bill Roston photograph.

THE NORTHERN PIKE has about the same appeal to fishermen as the wolf or the grizzly does to some big-game hunters. But while the rapacious nature of the two animals is grossly exaggerated, old *Esox lucius*, the waterwolf, is indeed a nasty customer—at least to foodfish, ducklings and the odd baby muskrat. The name itself comes from the fish's resemblance to the slim and deadly blade of that favorite medieval weapon. Early angling literature has many pike stories, mostly about monsters of dubious authenticity that would outstrip even world-class barracuda. However, the biggest pike still occur in northern Europe, where fifty-pounders are reported almost every year, and there are reasonably credible tales of seventy-pound Amur pike in Mongolia. So perhaps some of the legendary Irish and German monsters did exist. Few North American northerns exceed twenty-five pounds (despite Alaskan tales of giant "jackfish" that swallow canoes), but given the pike's long, slim body, such a fish makes a very respectable showing in a net. Originally found only north of about 60 degrees latitude, pike made their way into New England more than a century ago, and have since been transplanted throughout

A hooked muskellunge, photographed by Doug Stamm.

A muskellunge moves through its hunting grounds, photographed by Doug Stamm.

A rare photograph of a free-swimming muskellunge, by Doug Stamm.

Northern pike—the waterwolf.
Photograph by Don Blegen.

Northern pike destined for the smoke-house. Photograph by Don Blegen.

Northern pike destined for the smoke-house. Photograph by Don Blegen.

A gigantic—and well-fed—fly-caught northern pike of about 16 kilos.

MASKALONGE (Lucius ohiensis (Kirtland))

THE PIKE. (Lucius Lucius. L.)

THE PICKEREL. (Lucius reticulatus. Le Sueur.)
FROM A POND IN MASSACHUSETTS.

A northern pike, the "waterwolf," turns to inspect the camera. Minnesota Dept. of Natural resources photograph.

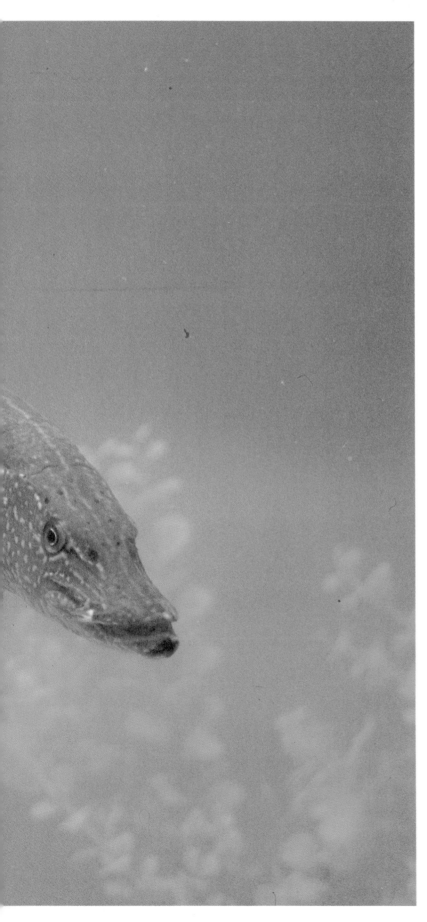

the Midwest and as far south as North Carolina.

(By contrast, the pike's smaller cousin, the chain pickerel, also an *Esox*, occurs naturally almost everywhere east of the Mississippi drainage. Too small to be considered "real" gamefish, the pickerel and its slashing strike has nevertheless hooked millions of kids on a lifetime of fishing.)

Pike like fairly still, fairly shallow water, often lying in motionless ambush under some sort of cover, waiting like a mugger for a little old lady with her Welfare. There are exceptions, as always. While wading a swift Labrador river, I almost stepped on a medium-sized pike that was lying in six inches of water in the lee of a rock; it had a ten-inch brook trout sideways in its jaws. The pike rolled one eye upward, studied me, then deliberately swallowed the trout down before shooting away into the current.

The way to take pike is by playing their game—swimming a baitfish imitation low and slow past their noses, or attracting them to the surface with a noisy top-water lure. They are sprinters; a pike will dash from its lie, clamp down on its target, and stop. Your lure will too. When you lean on the fish, what happens next depends on how big it is, but in any case the next few minutes can be spectacular. I've never seen pike jump, except on the strike (one launched itself right out of the water into a shallow racing dive in its hurry to fall on my "escaping" popper), but they'll try everything else. And they are tenacious: Several times I've boated pike that weren't even hooked—they had the fly in a deathgrip and just wouldn't let go. Pike teeth will tear up terminal tackle (and your fingers, if you're careless in unhooking them) in a hurry; the trick is to use long-bodied flies or lures, steel swivels and/or wire or heavy mono-filament shock tippets. And check your tackle after every strike.

There is another way to take pike, legal in very few places—by shooting them. In Vermont, for example, there's a ten-day spring season; northerns by the thousands spawn in the flooded shores of Lake Champlain, and a few diehard locals hunt them from canoes or on foot, in waders, bearing heavy-caliber handguns or shotguns loaded with slugs.

A spawning pike, especially a large female, is easily spotted by her dorsal fin sticking out of the water. As the pike's fin is very close to the tail, it takes keen judgement and a good eye to put a round into the muddy water next to the unseen head. The concussion kills or stuns the fish, which then floats belly-up. Pike taken this way are often smoked, which dissolves a number of the pesky little bones, and are delicious. A most bizarre and occasionally dangerous sport that, in the spooky, flooded forest, sometimes takes on the aspect of a jungle firefight.

There are still places where fishermen "release" pike by batting them across the water with canoe paddles, but in this day and age most of us recognize that predators, be they wolves or pike, are just as important as prey to the balance of nature. Live and let live goes for pike as well as for trout and salmon.

If you're after American "pike" of legendary old-world proportions, the **muskellunge** is your fish. Like all good monsters, it is fairly rare and has a restricted northeastern/upper midwestern range (helps build up the stories, you see), and it's, well, big. The IGFA recognizes a 70-pound musky caught in 1957 in New York's St. Lawrence River as the all-tackle record, but as always bigger, if unverified, specimens have been taken. For all intents and purposes, consider the musky an even-larger version of the northern pike, with dark markings— bars or spots— against a light body color, whereas the pike bears light oblong patches on a darker background. And where pike and pickerel have scales all over their cheeks (forward of the gill covers), the muskellunge's cheeks have scales only on the upper half, if at all. Fish-story-wise, take everything you've heard or seen about northern pike, magnify it, and you'll be prepared for muskies: If a pike could take your finger off, a musky could do your hand, and so on.

Fishing for muskies gets into people's blood. The musky's size— only king salmon, sturgeon and a few catfish are larger, in fresh water— and scarcity— Canadian biologists say that experienced musky fishermen average one hundred angling hours per legal fish— and dining habits— anything up to small beavers is fair game— put it in a class by itself. Musky fishermen call their sport a cat-and-mouse game, with man as the mouse.

Muskellunge have been caught on flies, but the experts use heavy baitcasting tackle rigged with huge topwater plugs. Because big muskies seem rare even in good water, locating their lies is as important as it is to the trophy brown-trout fisherman. (I say the fish *seem* rare, but what I mean is that hookups are rare; no one knows how many lures a big old musky ignores before finally lunging after one.) Working shallow, weedy shorelines, drop your plug into the water so that it seems to be struggling toward the safety of land or cover, and then crank it on home. Give it lots of life by jigging your rod tip and varying the retrieve speed. Don't let it stop long enough for Mr. Musky to get a good look at it; let him see only action— bubbles, blurs, drunken dives and staggers. The fish may follow you right to the boat before striking, or it may not strike at all, just hanging momentarily in the water a rod length away before vanishing from sight.

Stunning as this can be, the most overcome is usually the bass or panfish angler who unwittingly drops his lure on top of a hungry musky. To be suddenly attacked by something roughly the size, shape, disposition and speed of a cruise missile can provoke cardiac stutters.

Although there are many local names for this gamefish, science recognizes only one species, the muskellunge, and one variant, the **tiger musky**. This strikingly striped predator is a hybrid, the offspring of a northern pike and a muskellunge, and is considered the catch of a lifetime by many fishermen. Like a mule. the tiger musky is sterile. So if by some fantastic stroke of luck you hook and boat a tiger approaching the all-tackle record of 51 pounds 3 ounces, by all means knock it on the head and have it mounted, for it can't make little tigers even if you do let it go.

A very fine specimen of Canadian northern pike. Jim Lardner, The In-Fisherman, photograph.

It takes a large net to swallow twenty-five pounds of northern pike. The fish is still chewing the tinsel fly that fooled it. Author's photograph.

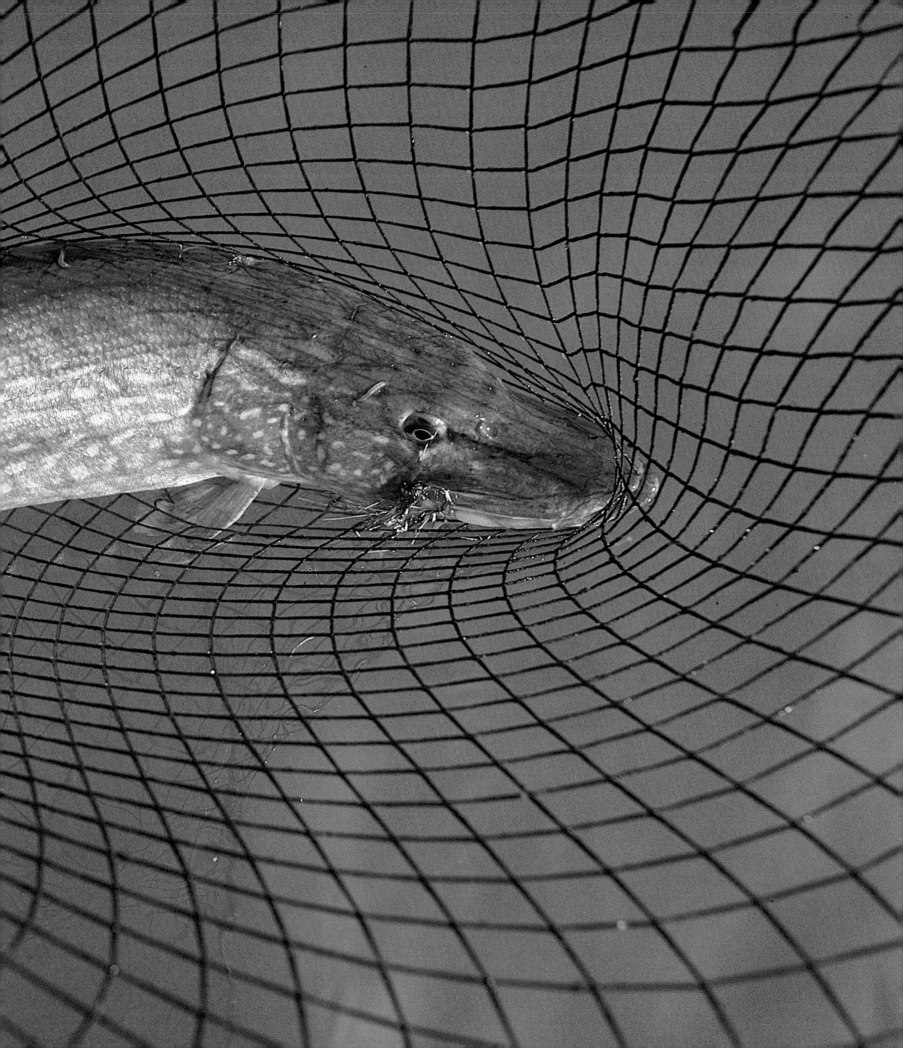

Sea-Run Fish

Salmo salar, the Atlantic salmon. Author's photograph.

THE SALMON, an anadromous fish, has grown up at sea, feeding upon seemingly limitless shoals of herring, small crabs, squid, and plankton such as krill and shrimp. Barring encounters with commercial fishermen and a few other predators, life is grand out in the open ocean—there's room to roam, and little to cramp this fish's bold style. But in two or three years, or five or more in some individuals, an age-old hunger draws the salmon out of the infinite, safe deeps and launches them upon a journey few will survive. The need to spawn, to reproduce the species, to keep the eternal cycle going, urges the salmon toward shore to find their home river.

Relying on a sense of smell/taste far keener than any scientific instrument yet built by man, salmon home in on minute traces of fresh river water mingling with the sea. As they enter the estuaries they swam out of several years earlier as young smolts, their troubles begin. As the coast begins to embrace the salmon within its headlands, the seals increase. Fishing boats find them easily and corner the schools with their nets. In the rivermouths the bottom shoals rapidly and even hungry seabirds

A still-bright male silver salmon caught in the far Northwest.

A fly-caught northwestern silver salmon at the peak of its spawning cycle; the "silver" has become fiery red.

A Great Lakes chinook, or king salmon. Photograph by Doug Stamm.

A hooked Great Lakes chinook, its mouth and jaw tangled after a long battle. Photograph by Doug Stamm.

A chum salmon, its spawning duty done, expires in the shallows of a northwestern river.

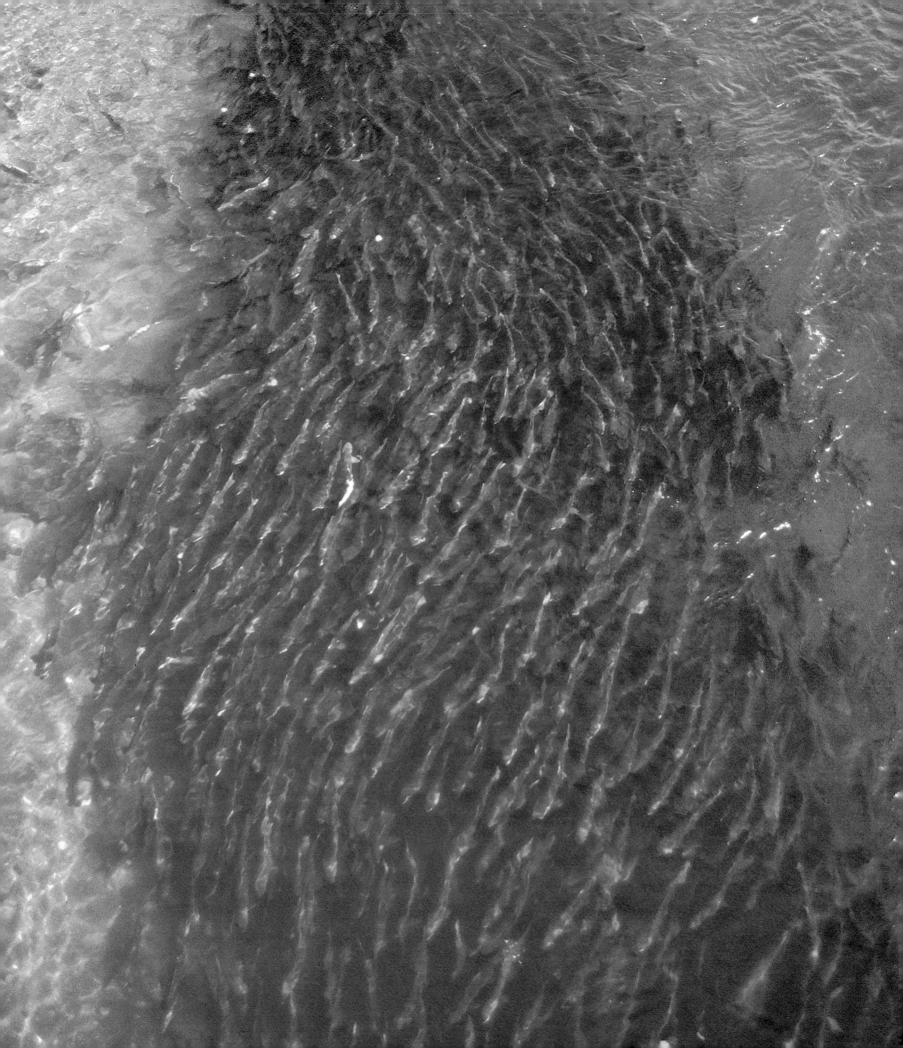

Preceding page:
A spectacular "run" of Alaskan sock-
eye salmon, migrating upstream to
spawn in late summer. David Lam-
broughton photograph.

A prime, bright-silver coho salmon
fresh from the Pacific Ocean and about
to be released back into its spawning
river. David Lambroughton photo-
graph.

Atlantic salmon resting deep in a pool on their way up Quebec's Grand Cascapedia River to spawn. Gilbert van Ryckevorsel photograph.

can now reach the fish. The salmon that survive pass up into the still-narrower confines of their streams and rivers, and the predation begins in earnest.

Otters, mink, fisher cats, ospreys and eagles. In the far Northwest, the great brown bears have been waiting since they emerged from their winter dens for the salmon to appear. And man is there too—man the netter, man the poacher, and man the angler.

Little wonder then that the salmon—grown outlandishly strong in the wide sea, now hemmed in by streambanks, forced to combat swift river currents, unable to eat, and diverted from the spawning imperative by predators of every sort—becomes a tiger on rod and line, a champion battler for freedom. A freshwater gamefish without superior and with few equals.

Along the Northeastern coast, from the Connecticut River and along the St. Lawrence to the northern capes of Newfoundland and Ungava Bay, the returning fish are **Atlantic salmon**. Here sportsmen may take them only by fly-fishing, a tradition that harkens back more than a century to the beginnings of salmon sportfishing in Britain. An Atlantic salmon is at least three years old, perhaps six or in rare cases seven years old when it first returns to fresh water in late spring and summer. It may be as small as ten pounds or as large as forty or more pounds, depending on genetic traits and time and conditions at sea. Upon entering its river, each salmon is shiny bright, carrying perhaps a sprinkling of irregular black markings on its sides and darker back. If sea lice are still attached to the fish, it has been out of salt water only a few hours.

The salmon have returned to spawn, and *only* to spawn. They will not, and cannot, eat at all; their metabolisms have changed, diverting energy from the digestive organs to the sexual organs.

This then is the eternal question facing the salmon fisherman: How to lure a fish that won't eat to a "baited" hook? Theories are that salmon strike a fly out of curiosity; out of aggression, to defend themselves or their mate or their nest; or through a conditioned response, an instinctive surrender to a sequence of events that a month earlier meant food. No matter the why, the most successful salmon anglers are those who have learned a river well enough to pinpoint, even in high, dark water, the lies where the migrating fish rest—the rocks, snags, ledges and shelves of the river bottom itself that break the current. Salmon consistently hole up in the same spots on their way upstream, and a fly swum just so through their "window" of visibility will bring a strike.

Or it may not. Like everyone who's fished for salmon, I've spent hours and even days casting long to holding fish: I can see the torpedo shapes in the water when the light is right, but I know they're there also because often, as if to egg me on, a fish rolls mightily on the surface, which makes my knees turn to sponge rubber. All ignore my fly no matter how many times I change pattern, size and the depth and speed at which the fly swims. Then, when my patience is gone and frustration gets the upper hand, I fling out one more last cast and rip it back through the water, my mind already on home or the next pool. Sure enough—out of the corner of my eye I see a swirl, a broad back rise through the surface, then feel a solid bump on my line—but that's all, because I was mentally gone, my concentration broken. Stupid SOB! Won't I ever learn?

As water flow and temperatures permit, small bands of salmon struggle "home," sometimes winning their way a hundred miles or more upstream until they reach a pool with the right combination of current and substrate. The hen fish selects a spot and, holding herself almost flat to the bottom, sends the gravel flying with powerful strokes of her broad tail. With the aid of the current she soon has scoured out a large, shallow redd, or nest, in which she deposits her eggs. The male fish takes his turn, fertilizing the eggs with a cloud of milt, and then the hen goes back to work, covering the eggs with new gravel she digs from just upstream. In so doing, she creates another redd and often uses that as well, eventually laying some 7,000 to 20,000 eggs.

The fingerlings hatch soon and like their parents they overwinter in the river. The mature fish that have survived these months in fresh water—still without feeding—are called kelts, or black salmon, and they are pitifully thin and dark. Still facing upriver as though heeding the echo of the spawning urge, they allow the spring currents to push them back to the sea, where a fortunate few feed and grow and regain their strength for another run. The salmon young, first called parr, pass their first two or three years in the river until, as smolts of maybe eight inches, they too head for the salt.

Estimates are that maybe only ten percent of Atlantic salmon survive to spawn a second time. A very few ac-

A pair of grilse, small Atlantic salmon, legally killed for the smokehouse. Author's photograph.

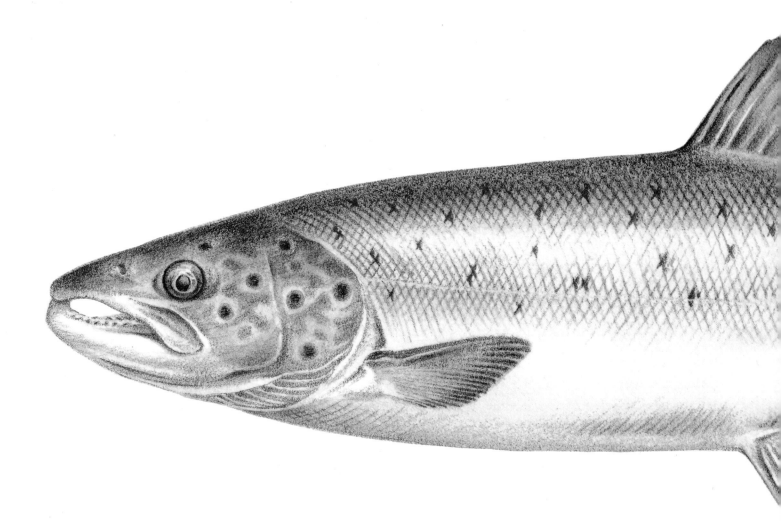

complish this three and perhaps even four times.

Thanks to restrictions on commercial netters, North American salmon populations have rebounded somewhat in the last decade. Efforts are under way also to transplant Atlantics into some Great Lakes streams, and much time and money is being spent on restoring the salmon rivers of New England, with growing success. The catch in Maine's Penobscot River (in pools in downtown Bangor!) approaches a thousand fish every year. Canadian Atlantic salmon fishing is still often regarded as a blue-blood sport, but as the fishing improves the many miles of public water do too. Some of the best salmon water in the world is now available to anyone with a week's vacation, a car and enough cash to swing a few days' camping. As the emphasis swings away from private water, and as new catch-and-release

regulations take effect, a new breed of salmon angler is developing—younger, more conservation-minded, more attuned to current trends in angling.

Lee Wulff, the greatest American salmon angler, likens the fish in fresh water to an electric battery. Charged with energy from its seasons at sea, it must survive without food for almost a year. The angler who hooks one, plays it and releases it has drawn down that charge, forced the fish to spend some of its vital strength. And so it is doubly important that the fisherman play the salmon well, to avoid injuring it directly (by hooking it elsewhere than in the mouth or by dragging it onto sand or rocks to land it) and to avoid playing it too long. Many fishermen now use special leaders between fly and line that let them break off a salmon that can't be landed within an acceptably short time span. A good gamefish, said Lee Wulff

many years ago, is too valuable to be caught only once.

The **landlocked salmon** is about identical to the Atlantic salmon; it's simply not able to go to sea because of physical barriers—a dam, for example, either natural or manmade. Therefore it substitutes a deep, clear, cold lake for the ocean in which to mature, and then in the fall the landlock swims up into a tributary stream or river to go through the same spawning ritual.

It is now known that after the most recent glaciation, which withdrew from New England about 10,000 years ago, large populations of such freshwater salmon were established in Labrador, Newfoundland, and New Brunswick and Quebec, and as far inland as Lake Ontario. However, overfishing, pollution, dams and habitat destruction shrank the range of the landlocked to Maine and to eastern Canada, where the fish is called the *ouananiche*.

Recognizing the value of this somewhat unique gamefish, the state of Maine has been researching landlocked-salmon biology since 1868. And with some success, too: Maine salmon eggs and fry have to date been transplanted to the waters of some two dozen other states and foreign countries, and now landlocks are once again found throughout the Northeast into Michigan.

Bowing to scientific evidence, the IGFA (the International Game Fish Association, which keeps modern sportfishing records) not long ago did away with the separate category for landlocked salmon in its record books, combining it instead with its near-twin, the Atlantic salmon. Because the sea-run variety is inevitably larger, this meant that the grand twenty-two-plus-pound landlocked caught in Maine's Sebago Lake in 1907 was disqualified as a

An Alaskan chum, or dog, salmon—so-called because the native people netted them to feed to their sled dogs over the winters—beginning to turn spawning red. Author's photograph.

salmon record. To the thousands of passionate landlocked fishermen of New England, this was a blow to their pride—henceforth they would have to regard their premier gamefish as nothing more than a scaled-down Atlantic. But there are worse fates; and like the sea-run salmon, the landlocked is a gamefish in every sense—strong and fast, an aerial battler that readily comes to an artificial.

Summers on the lakes of Northern New England, landlocked-salmon fishermen often troll streamer flies or bright spoons or even sewn bait slowly behind their canoes or guideboats. In late spring, when water temperatures are still cool, the salmon often come to the surface to chase baitfish or take hatching insects, and then casting can be rewarding. Every fall, when the spawn begins, landlockeds can be taken in moving water, with the techniques stream trout fishermen use, and this is the climax of the season. But a hot, dry fall may keep the salmon in the lakes until after the legal season shuts down. Fisherman's luck, it's called.

On the Northern Pacific Coast of this continent there are not one but five species of salmon that crowd up into the rivers every summer to lay their eggs. In addition to this variety, and the fact that western salmon don't specifically seek out their birth river, there's another important distinction between these fish and their East-Coast cousins: Pacifics, all of them, die in spectacularly messy fashion after their first and only spawn.

The five Pacific salmon each have at least two popular names, which does nothing to unconfuse fishermen. One set are the names you see on cans of eating salmon, the other is generally the "sporting" names. The biggest and least plentiful of the Pacifics, and one of the most valuable for market and for sport, is the chinook, also known as the **king salmon**.

Found from Northern California up to the Bering Strait, kings are the largest of the salmon and trout family in North America. The current IGFA all-tackle record for kings is a 97-pound four-ounce behemoth that was taken from Alaska's Kenai River in 1985, but there are reliable reports of 120-plus-pounders captured in commercial nets. There are spring, summer and fall runs, but kings are generally the first of the five Pacific salmon to arrive in fresh water, reaching Alaska's Bristol Bay, for example, in June. There, as the spring runoff drops and the streams clear up, these fish become visible—very visible, thanks to their size. Fishermen accustomed to sixteen-inch trout go into mild hysteria the first time they spot a mating pair of these nuclear subs cruising upstream, leaving a wake in four feet of water. To see them approaching while you're wading a small river is to experience the urge to get out of the water and let them pass.

Sheer size and power make them a top gamefish, but of course they're harmless. Still, the worst fright I ever got while fishing was courtesy of a king salmon. A friend and I were fishing a high and muddy Alaskan river, wading deep and casting long, letting our streamer flies swing downstream in the current before retrieving them. Carl was just upriver of me and he was the first to hook up. He yelled "Strike!" I turned to look at him and something unseen in the water cannoned into my knees. Only the level bottom kept me from going in over my head. I staggered back, let out a howl and backpedaled for shore virtually on top of the water. A salmon surfaced in the spot I'd vacated, thrashing frantically against Carl's line. It turned out to be a chinook of only seventeen pounds.

Like all sea-run fish, kings are usually bright upon entering fresh water and over the next month they lose their sheen, turning darker and redder week by week. Males sport tremendous kypes, the hooked lower jaw characteristic of salmonids. Pods of kings work their way upstream for weeks, traveling as much as two thousand miles in the Yukon River. In smaller water they move erratically, resting in the deeper pools, swimming steadily through the channels, gathering below the riffles to take their turn powering through these risky shallows, sometimes with half their bodies showing above the surface. At the headwaters they split up into pairs and sometimes fade back into tiny feeder streams no wider than the fish are long, where they dig their redds and deposit and fertilize their eggs.

Then they die, each and every one.

In the large king rivers such as the Columbia and the Kenai, fishing with heavy tackle from shore or boats is effective, trolling or casting blindly and at long range to cover lots of water. But stalking big kings on foot in small wilderness streams is one of few fishing experiences that give me buck fever. In water so clear you can see the action, you jig your lure or fly past the noses of resting salmon. When one of them moves forward and your line just stops in the water—maybe you've seen the flash of the fish's mouth opening briefly—it's time to set the hook. Hard. Several times. These big ones have a manner reminiscent of a Panama-Canal-class bulldozer, and hooking onto one on light tackle is a straining experience. Twenty or twenty-five pounds is an average size, and they are tough fighters, but the truly big kings, twice that size and more, will stand your hair on end. Even after many weeks in fresh water they keep their strength, and use it well. When you drive the hook home, a big king will often surface (to size up his enemy?), and the sight will weaken your knees. Then you're in for an hour or more of running downstream, hard pulling, frantic reeling and involuntary yells, screams, curses and other expressions of awe as the fish dives, then thrashes on the surface, throwing spray into the treetops with a tail like a snow shovel. If you're very fortunate and make no mistakes, you may land him.

They are not accepted as "real" gamefish, but three of the other four Pacific salmons nevertheless give the angler a decent thrash on rod and reel. **Humpback** salmon—known also as pinks—are relatively small, slab-sided, with almost beak-like jaws and strongly humped shoulders, and excellent table fare when fresh and bright for campers who need a break from Spam. **Chum** salmon, whose other name is dog salmon (because northern native people netted them to feed their dogs in winter), are more plentiful in the lower rivers of western Canada and Alaska. They are bigger than humpies, generally ten to fifteen pounds or so, and alone of the Pacific salmons do not turn crimson to spawn. Instead they develop startling streaks of maroon that extend up their green sides like dull flames licking at a board. In spite of their reputation as "dogs," they will readily take lures and flies and fight for their survival.

The **sockeye**, or red salmon, is the most plentiful in the Northwest. Found from San Francisco northward, it's the one most likely to show up on the label of a can of salmon. It is no trophy even when fresh, but it can be spurred into striking a hook. The sockeye's chief benefit to sportfishermen (and to hunters, netters, conservationists and anyone else interested in preserving the Northwestern ecology) is the sheer size of the annual spawning run. Those millions of fish and the billions of eggs they lay every summer are the prime food source for many other gamefish and for other animals ranging from insects up through birds and foxes to the coastal grizzlies, the brown bears.

Eggs washed by current from the redds tumble downstream like large red BB shot, to the satisfaction of trout, Dolly Varden, grayling and sometimes northern pike that wait below with mouths open. Bears, seals and some birds take the live fish themselves. The salmon that live to spawn contribute too: When their eggs have been deposited, the weeks of hard swimming without food take their toll. By now the salmon are grotesques—thin, mottled red, with wildly humped backs and hooked jaws bristling with sharp teeth. Digestive organs have atrophied to nothing. Fins have worn away to stumps. The flesh seems to peel from their bones. Still struggling against the currents, they eventually turn turtle and hang up in the snags or wash up on the sandbars. Birds and insects pick the carcasses apart, beginning with the eyes. The meat eventually melts away, turning the rivers into protein soup for the microscopic organisms at the base of the food chain. On hot days the rivers may smell like garbage dumps, and the bones of thousands of salmon bleach in the shallows.

Though much smaller than the chinook, the **coho**, the fifth Pacific salmon, gets the vote as Number One Gamefish from many anglers. Its reputation as a hook-and-line battler has led to its successful transplantation into the Great Lakes and waters as far east as Lake Champlain and even a few coastal New England rivers. In its native northwestern rivers it's often known as the silver salmon, a handle that suits it well. In the estuaries or newly arrived in fresh water, these fish are chrome-plated beauties with speed to match. Silvers are extremely valuable fish, for they bring millions of dollars of sportfishing revenue into their regions.

A male humpbacked salmon, still sea-bright. David Lambroughton photograph.

An angler carefully unhooks a fly-caught British Columbia steelhead prior to release. David Lambroughton photograph.

Wherever you go to take them, the fishing is often the same: in streams that are low and clear—because silvers normally arrive in the second half of the summer—you look for the fish. They travel in groups of a dozen or so to maybe a hundred, never staying long in one spot and moving fast when under way. They don't swim far from salt water, though. Intercept them from upstream, make your spinner, spoon or streamer dance in front of them at the right depth, and a smash-and-grab strike is almost inevitable. Silvers rarely go bigger than about twelve pounds, which is both a shame and a bless-ng—they fight with berserk abandon,

and if they reached the size of Atlantic salmon, landing one might become a rare event.

When the silvers are in (a rallying cry, the fisherman's *Surf's Up!*), we sometimes get a little strange. I've watched anglers, particularly ones new to both silvers and the long days of the northern summer, fish until they were exhausted, staggering in the water to hook just one more, to feel the energy of another salmon exploding through the surface and cartwheeling away. Two dozen such hookups in a day will reduce any fisherman to jelly, blubbering but elated. Even as spawning approaches, and the hens turn bronzed and dark and the males go angry red, coho seem to keep their strength, although they do cut down on the aerobatics.

But no sea-run fish gets the kind of respect, if not awe, accorded to the **steelhead**. This is nothing more than a rainbow trout that has taken it into its genes to leave running water, mature at sea or in large lakes, and then return, like a salmon, to lay its eggs. But when you combine the natural style and looks of the river rainbow with the size, strength and feeding habits of a sea predator, you get a gamefish of Atlantic-salmon caliber. (Steelhead fans would put that the other way around, of course.) Like Atlantics, they may return to spawn more than once, but unlike them, they may arrive in their rivers in January as well as in July; there are two distinct strains—summer steelhead and winter steelhead. Both enter fresh water as slim, supercharged steely torpedoes, both darken and develop the rainbow's rose body stripe, until they look like oversize trout.

From northern California up to the Canadian line and in the Great Lakes tributaries, six to fifteen pounds is normal for steelhead, but in the wilds of coastal British Columbia, beware, for—as the old maps used to say—here lie monsters. A few steelhead approaching forty pounds are taken and released every year. Fishermen who go to the trouble and expense to catch such steelhead become emotionally involved with their quarry, and treat them with infinite care. Killing one intentionally is beyond them, and so few of these fish are ever recorded anywhere except on slide film or home video.

Compared to Pacific salmon, steelhead are almost rare, but a network of legal protection is slowly enveloping them. As with the Atlantic salmon, a mystique has grown up about steelhead fishing. These fish do eat—a little—while in their streams, but aggression and curiosity again seem to be the chief motivation behind strikes, even at bait. Summer-run fish often appear in low, clear water, and because they are spooky fish, they must be stalked carefully. On rivers like Oregon's Rogue and Umpqua, fly fishermen often resort to leaders of twelve feet or longer, to put the fly that much farther from the thick line. And long, fine leaders demand much fish-fighting ability from the angler if he ever hopes to land one of these rockets. (Unlike many sea-run fish, steelhead often develop the habit of ducking under snags and other cover when hooked, which doesn't help the fisherman one bit.) Although much steelheading with

FEMALE LAND LOCKED SALMON or QUANANICHE.
(Salmo Salar Sebago. Girard.)

flies calls for wet patterns fished below the surface, often on heavy shooting-taper lines that help cover water quickly, some Canadian rivers carry steelhead that are very willing to come to a large dry fly.

Other rivers, such as the Thompson, in British Columbia, are so big and so wild that fly-fishing is almost out of the question. Big spinning outfits put artificials out to the fish at much less risk to life and limb, but purists are now arming themselves with huge two-handed fly rods, in the European manner, and swimming their flies well even in such tough conditions.

Winter and spring steelheading is very popular, especially in the upper Midwest (although sizable transplants of summer-run fish have taken hold there). As the lake ice breaks up, steelhead cluster around the river mouths, waiting for the slight rise in water temperature that triggers their migration. This seems a particularly masochistic form of sport—wading bone-chilling water, casting in snow and winter wind, numbed fingers trying to chip ice from the line guides—but it's not that different from duck hunting at the same northern latitudes.

A common summer sight in coastal Alaskan streams—"reds" moving up-river to spawn, all but oblivious of predators ranging from bears to fishermen. R. Valentine Atkinson photograph.

Following spread:
Fifty-plus pounds of Alaskan king salmon, taken on a medium-weight fly rod. Some Bristol Bay kings turn red even before swimming up into fresh water. Author's photograph.

Shad

HICKORY SHAD (POMOLOBUS MEDIOCRIS)

SO THE SHAD is nothing more than an overgrown herring? Well, on the northeastern coast of the United States, where they know the difference, this silver sea-run fish is often regarded as the poor man's Atlantic salmon. Times have changed, though. Now even comparatively poor (that is, un-rich) fishermen have access to top salmon waters; and even the well-to-do angler knows not to discount the humble shad as a gamefish.

Springtime, when the shadbush blooms white, look for the annual spawning runs to start in coastal rivers around the country. The hickory shad, with its underslung lower jaw, is the southern cousin; although it does reach New England, most of the run is south of the Chesapeake. Like all fish that have spent time at sea, hickories are tough fighters, but they are normally only a couple of pounds. Most popular among sportfishermen is the American shad (white shad), which is commonly five to eight pounds and sometimes goes over ten.

American shad are native to the East Coast, where they range from Maine to Florida. But Seth Green, America's favorite fish planter, brought shad to the West Coast in 1871. He dumped the fry into the Sacramento River, and now they're found from Baja California to Alaska! Northern shad typically spawn more than once, and willingly enter rivers other than their birthplace, so this is a dependably plentiful fishery—at least for the Lower 48, with its dams and pollution.

The top shad rivers are probably the Delaware and the Connecticut, on the East Coast. (The Hudson gets a strong run too, but it is too big to fish easily with rod and reel; small commercial netting outfits take many Hudson shad.) On both coasts the shad runs are virtually social occasions; there are shad festivals, offering lessons in de-boning and filleting the fish, and tasty planked shad and shad roe dishes. But *the* classic shad fishery is the mob scene that takes place below the Enfield Dam, on the Connecticut in Connecticut. Fishermen line up elbow-to-ribs along the concrete spillways, casting lead-head shad darts to the thousands of fish that mill around in frustration, trying to pass upriver. Pandemonium reigns when a fish strikes and cuts across a dozen other lines. Out in the river small boats zoom around, trying to locate the fish channels. Some of the most successful anglers are the brave souls in chest waders who struggle against the swift water and the slippery, unpredictable ledge bottom—if you've got the heart for it, and can anchor yourself slightly upstream and alongside of one of the runs where the fish come through, you can take a shad an hour on a fly or lure. You must find the depth and the slot where the fish want it, and keep your offering there, jigging it occasionally to provoke an aggressive or defensive strike.

But a fish hooked is not a fish landed. Shad have soft mouths and broad, powerful sides that they use effectively in the strong current. Best is to fish with a partner; let him move downstream of you, then drop the fish into his waiting net before the hook pulls out. I am very fond of shad roe and keep a few large hen fish. But one of the largest I lost when the river simply tore the carcass off my belt stringer.

A hickory shad, interrupted on its annual upstream spawning migration. Joel Arrington photograph.

Sheefish

ABOUT ALL most of us know about the **sheefish** is that it's usually subtitled "the tarpon of the North." Well, its real name is *inconnu*, or "the unknown." Doesn't help much, does it? Because they are scattered in the rivers and lakes of arctic Canada and in Alaska above the Kuskokwim, few of us ever get a crack at a sheefish, much less catch one. Unknown, indeed.

But prized, and for this same rarity. Anglers who keep a life-list of their catches tend to regard sheefish the way many big-game hunters think of, say, Marco Polo sheep: *Someday I'll get one!*

The facts, however, are these: The sheefish is a genuine salmonid, a whitefish in fact (biologists invariably point out that it is the only *predatory* whitefish), but it does bear a marked resemblance to a tarpon—large, silvery scales, stubbornly outthrust lower jaw, long, slim, powerful body, all wrapped up in a pugnacious package that's quite willing to take a hook and bust up the river. Also like the tarpon, there's something primitive about sheefish, some echo of the prehistoric past. They're salmonids, yes, but they seem to be salmonids whose evolution somehow stopped an age or two ago, leaving them behind their peer group. Like salmon, they spawn in the fall and they swim hundreds of miles upstream to do so, but they don't come in from the sea; they mature in the fresh water of their rivermouths. And like salmon they deposit their eggs on the riverbottoms, but they're broadcast spawners—the female digs no redd, just pumps her spawn into the water. Individual eggs (the ones that aren't eaten) eventually settle between the rocks, where they may or may not be fertilized by a cloud of milt fired off by one of the male fish. Tough-fighting and rough-edged, sheefish always make me think of rowdy dropouts who stayed in the old neighborhood a million years ago while their classmates went on to Darwin U. to become sophisticated salmon.

If you can catch trout, you know how to catch sheefish; you just have to get to the right water and then you have to play the odds, for they are not as numerous as most Alaskan or Canadian gamefish. They are called northern tarpon not only for their looks but also because they jump when hooked, even the big ones of thirty and forty pounds. But as far as I know, such behavior occurs only in streams where the water is skinny; hook a big sheefish in a lake and it'll head for the depths. In any event, you'll be glad you went.

The Alaskan sheefish. These were taken from the Kobuk River, which flows into Kotzebue Sound, western Alaska, just above the Arctic Circle. Ken Alt, Northern Alaska Fisheries Service, photograph.

Trout

THE BRITISH, bless 'em, did more to spread their sort of fishing (and shooting) sports than probably any other group of people on this planet. In Victorian times and earlier, with a disregard for other fish and animal species that would be appalling in today's enlightened society, British military men and commercial travelers and fortune-seekers—those who spent long periods of time away from their homeland—transplanted "their" trout and salmon and gamebirds and red deer and so on all over the planet. While assuring ourselves that *we* would never be so ecologically insensitive—at least now—we may heave a sigh of relief that *they* were, and proceed to enjoy the fruits of their labors.

But bringing fish and animals to North America would be like bringing extra sand to the beach; there was already an eye-popping variety here. Take the noble trout, for example. Of the nine or so true trout on this continent today, only one came from Britain. The trout we most value—the most sought-after as a trophy, conceded, rightly or not, to be the most difficult to catch and thus the best proof of a fisherman's skill—is the **brown trout**, an immigrant from Scotland. The descendants of those fish (brought to America in 1885) are still sometimes classified as Loch Leven browns.

More properly, however, many of our stream-living brown trout, though of European origin, did *not* come from the United Kingdom. While many older anglers still know them as German browns, that designation came into disfavor, for reasons that should be obvious, in the early 1940s. And they were indeed German—the first shipment of their eggs was sent to a hatchery in Long Island, New York, in 1883 by Baron Lucius von Behr.

In April 1984 the centennial anniversary of the first successful planting of these von Behr browns was celebrated by historically accurate reenactment. Members of the Izaak Walton League deposited, from a milk can, two thousand trout fry into the North Branch of Michigan's Pere Marquette River, near the town of Baldwin. On April 11, a

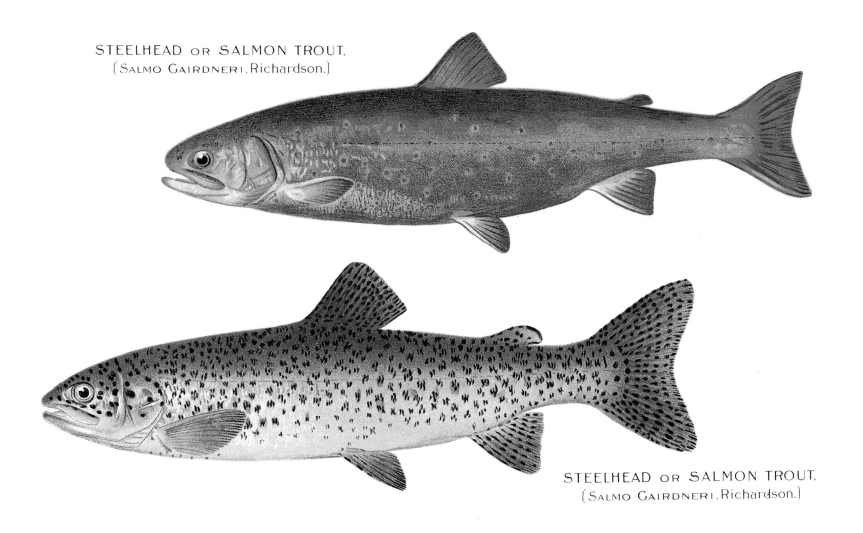

STEELHEAD or SALMON TROUT.
(Salmo Gairdneri, Richardson.)

STEELHEAD or SALMON TROUT.
(Salmo Gairdneri, Richardson.)

century earlier, a certain J.F. Ellis and his assistant, using milk cans, had transferred almost five thousand brown trout fry from a U.S. Fish Commission railcar into the cold, slightly tannic flow of the North Branch. American trout fishing, as has often been said, was changed forever.

The Loch Leven trout, as their name implies, were a stillwater strain, silvery as salmon at certain seasons. The German fish bore the red and black spots and the yellow flanks that today identify a brown trout to us. The two subspecies have interbred, however, as all trout can, and variations among North American browns are generally more due to environmental differences than to genetic traits.

A brown trout in spawning dress is a sight to behold, a gaudy gold and green, red and silver. Larger males develop spectacularly hooked jaws that, in com-

bination with the well-fed brown's broad shoulders and deep body, give them an aggressive appearance. This bullish look is borne out by the way they fight when hooked, often diving deep and slugging it out with massive head-shakings and dodging under snags and around river rocks. Like all trout, both stream- and lake-living browns feed primarily on aquatic insects, which makes them a prime quarry for the fly fisherman. But the larger fish have learned to find protein in bigger chunks— they've become cannibals, ambushing and eating smaller trout, leeches, shiners and other baitfish. (That's how they got so big.) These fish are much more difficult to take on flies, and now the lure and bait fisherman enjoys the upper hand. A large Rapala carefully retreived through a deep, still stream pool represents exactly what such a fish looks for.

100

A Rocky Mountain brown trout about to be released back into its habitat.

A small, but beautifully colored, Labrador brook trout.

A Canadian Kamloops trout, photographed by David Lambroughton.

Labrador guide Ray Best shows off a brightly colored three-kilo brook trout from Ann-Marie Lake in the Minipi River.

A small lake trout comes aboard. Photograph by Doug Stamm.

A spectacularly colored Alaskan "leopard" rainbow trout, with the leech-pattern streamer fly that fooled it still in its jaw.

A subarctic Dolly Varden, showing but hints of the spawning colors to come.

A fat, healthy wild brown trout from the Intermountain West. David Lam-broughton photograph.

Preceding spread:
A twelve-inch brown trout working steadily in his feeding lane. Dale Spartas photograph.

A heavily spotted Alaska "leopard" rainbow trout, th caribou-hair mouse fly that too it still stuck in its wood-har jaw. Author's photograph.

A silvery, lightly marked West-Coast rainbow trout. Contrast this fish with the rainbow on the facing page; variations in color, size and shape may exist from one river's population to the next when barriers keep species from intermingling. David Lam-broughton photograph.

An American classic-the native Western rainbow trout. Jim & KittyVincent photograph.

In friendly comparisons, when every judgement of speed and color and fighting ability has been made, brown-trout fans eventually play their trump card—that browns, especially those big ones, are caught far less often than rainbows or brookies. Which makes them more of a challenge, a truly superior gamefish. There's some truth to this, but remember that unlike their two popular cousins browns are generally nighttime feeders, while we are generally daytime anglers. Think back to the really monstrous browns you've seen, in newspaper photos or brought dripping into tackle shops on opening day: weren't most taken in the black of night, or by snot-nosed kids fishing deep with nightcrawlers? There's a lesson to be learned here.

Rainbow trout, by contrast, are native Yankees, although Westerners who were moved East (not to mention all over the rest of the planet, from Argentina to New Zealand to Europe) as their sterling qualities became known. Unlike many salmonids, wild rainbows are generally springtime spawners. They also cross-breed readily with other species, and of all the trouts accept the widest range of water temperatures and quality. This makes the rainbow the darling of the biologists and has led to many hybrids and sub-subspecies and hatchery experiments. The nonfishing public who sees trout only on a plate, garnished with lemon, would recognize the rainbow; many frozen supermarket trout are 'bows, often reared, harvested and flash-frozen in the Orient. And stream trout these days are often hatchery rainbows, pale, cookie-cutter fish mass-produced and released annually to satisfy the increasing demands of the fishing public. It's a testament to the rainbow's style that even these fish

THE CANADIAN RED TROUT
FEMALE

strike a fly or lure (or baited hook) with a certain dash.

But a wild rainbow is a gamefish to be reckoned with—a hunter that pounces like a cat and then gyrates wildly away across the top of the water when insulted with a hook. In fact, in western Alaska there's a strain of rainbows so heavily spotted and so predatory they are called leopard trout. The name fits. Some of the finest fishing I've had was there, twitching a caribou-hair mouse across the shallow coastal streams, swinging the fly out from the bank like a real mouse trying desperately to reach the far shore. A hungry rainbow would accelerate away, betraying its lie under the bank with a sudden swirl, and arc out into the current after the mouse, engulfing it from behind with its wide, white open mouth showing clearly against the green water. But some trout seemed to want to play, charging the struggling "mouse" five or six times before leaping upon it, sometimes even slapping it clear out of the water with their tails.

The trout's namesake rainbow is the slash of color that decorates its flanks.

This may be a wide band of stunning hot pink or just a pale rosy track or simply an irregular boundary between zones of spots on the fish's back and sides. The rest of the fish may be deep green above, fading through yellow to a white belly, patterned with irregular black specks, or—particularly near salt water—blazing silver with hardly any specks at all. Rainbows can show remarkable variation from one river or lake to another, never mind from region to region and season to season, and there are dozens of different strains. Some migrate readily to open water such as lakes or even the sea, others remain resident in their rivers year-round. And the potential for tremendous growth is there too: Canadian fisheries biologists report netting a rainbow of more than 52 pounds in a lake in British Columbia.

THE CANADIAN RED TROUT
ADULT MALE

The connoisseur's choice, however, may be the seemingly shy and retiring **brook trout**. Another American, the brookie evolved in the northeastern corner of the continent, and is considered the native trout from Labrador down through New England and into the southern Appalachians. Because the brookie was the only trout in New England before the 1880s, and New England, as the oldest white-settled region of America, was the birthplace of American fly-fishing, the brook trout figures heroically in our sportfishing history. Records from the 19th Century indicate that "squaretails" of eight and nine pounds were taken every year in the States; but today, even in the remote streams and lakes of northern Maine, a three-pounder makes the local newspapers.

It's a judgement call, but I think the brook trout is the most beautiful of America's gamefish. Delicate and jewel-like in small sizes, awesome and powerful as large fish, brookies are spectacularly colored—aquatic versions of the male wood duck. Their lower fins are red-gold, edged in black and white, and in male fish, particularly at spawning time, this color extends up onto their bellies. Their green-black backs are handsomely decorated with wavy lighter markings, and scattered along their lateral lines are handfuls of red or purple dots within blue halos.

Brook trout are not, of course, "shy and retiring"; merely finicky, demanding cleaner and colder water than other trout. As land is developed, clean, cold waters often become dirty and warmer, and resident brook trout move upstream to the headwaters and then, sometimes, die out. Even under environmental protection, fish grow more slowly in colder water and so it is relatively easy to clean out even a healthy brook trout fishery if angling pressure is high and fish are not released.

Another true native American, the brook trout. Don Blegen photograph.

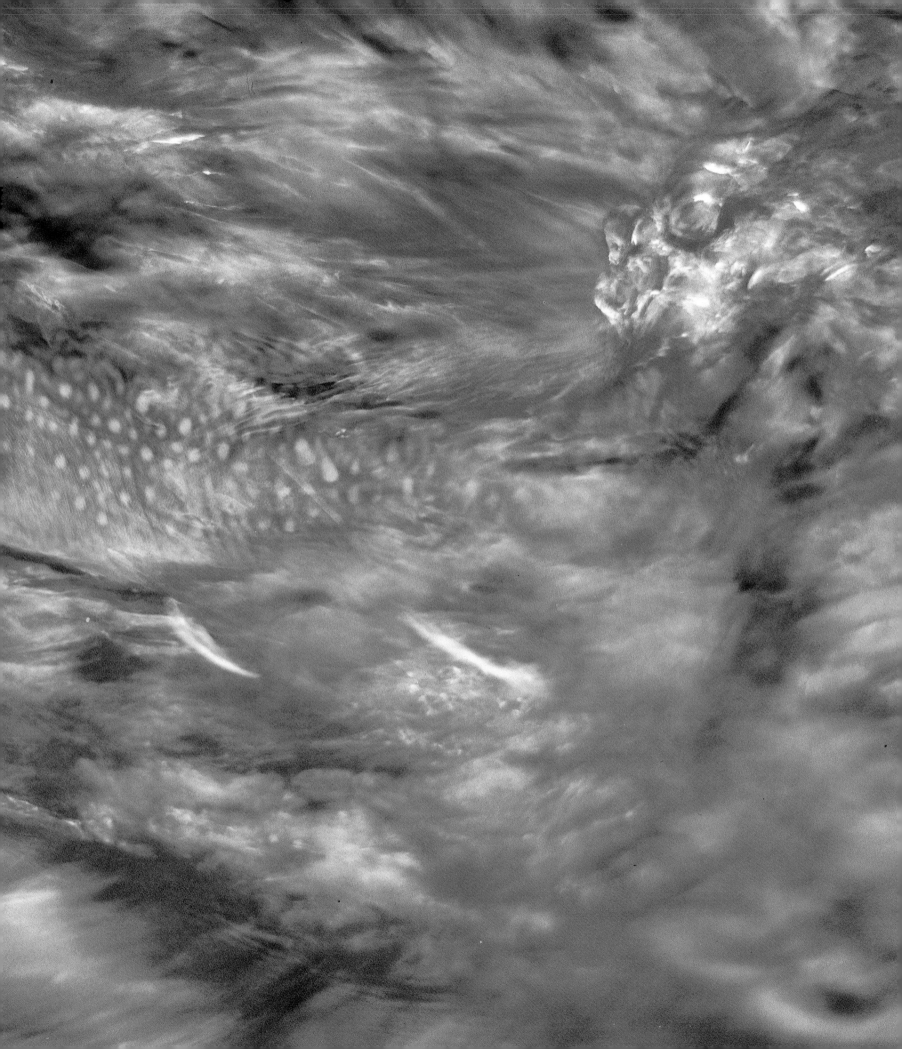

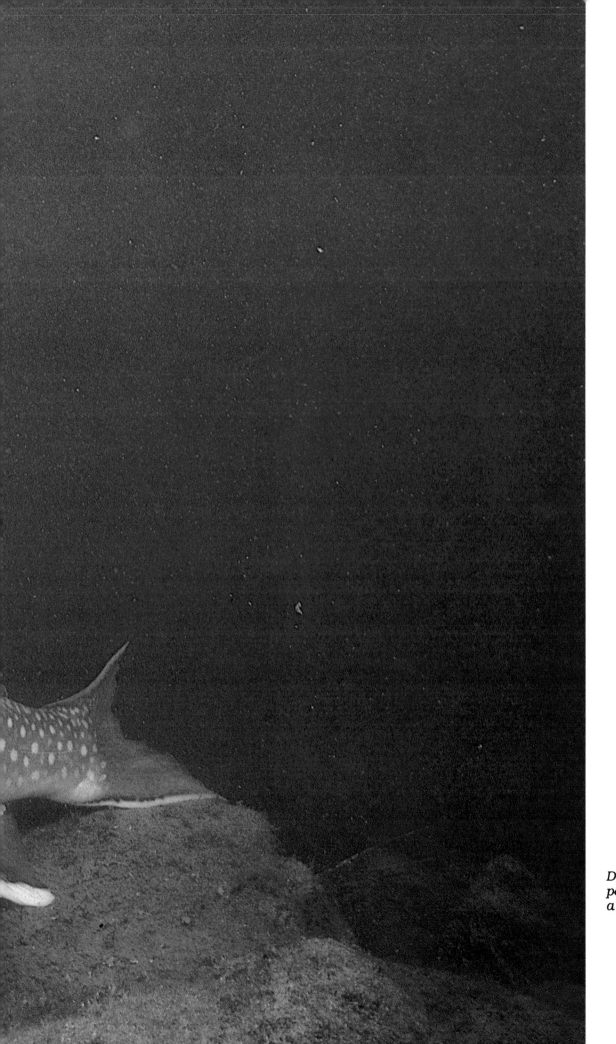

Diver Bill Roston photographed this perfectly marked brook trout charging a fly in a Virginia mountain pond.

In beaver ponds, especially newer ones that haven't silted in yet, you may find hundreds of hungry brook trout willing to compete fiercely for your hook no matter what's on it. This leads to the feeling that the brookie is too dumb for its own good, too ready to sample a lure or bait. However, having been snubbed by many big brook trout, even in unfished wilderness waters, I don't subscribe to this slander at all. Generations of kids have passed their summers dangling worms for eight-inch brookies in the rockbound pools of tiny mountain streams, but truly big brook trout are found in truly big waters. Today's world-record (nine pounds plus) brook trout come from Labrador's Minipi River and Quebec's Broadback watershed, where the "pools" are often lakes connected by short stretches of flowing stream. On calm summer evenings you'll find half a dozen or more brook trout feeding leisurely on huge mayflies. As their backs and dorsal fins arch above the surface, you realize that every one of them is almost as long as your arm. The slightly condescending "brookie" suddenly seems inappropriate.

In the Rocky Mountains the term "native trout" applies to the **cutthroat**, a species that appears in a variety of different forms and colors, each named for its region. Many anglers know the Yellowstone cutthroat and the Snake River cutts, but there are also strong cutthroat populations on the West Coast, from California up through British Columbia into Alaska, some of which spend part of their lives at sea, returning like salmon to lay their eggs in rivers, and some of which stay in fresh water. (Other recognized and officially classified strains of cutthroat include the Westslope, Humboldt, Paiute, Greenback, Bonneville, Rio Grande, Colorado River, Lahontan and Willow Creek.) Like most rainbows, cutthroat trout spawn in the spring; biologically they may in fact be closer to rainbows than to other trout, as the two species interbreed readily.

The lurid name comes not from any Jack-the-Ripper feeding (or mating!) tendencies but from the red-orange markings, often a vivid slash, behind and below the cutthroat's lower jaw. On some fish, particularly Yellowstone cutts, the marking is much more than a simple slash, extending upward into a red blush that covers almost the entire opercle, or "cheek."

Even cutthroat partisans concede that their fish is not a premier fighter or spectacular jumper on rod and reel, but it is nevertheless a worthy gamefish that can be taken on a variety of tackle. Like the brook trout, cutthroat sometimes suffer from a reputation for airheadedness, a suicidal willingness to take lure or bait. I invite people who believe that to fish any stillwater section of, say, the Yellowstone River, where big (*big*) cutthroat will rise majestically from their lies, inspect your offering with the deliberation of arms negotiators, then smugly sink back to the bottom, where they will go on feeding leisurely on nymphs and other naturals. In fast water cutthroats can be a piece of cake, but in those conditions, when a fish has only a split second to inspect any passing item that might be food, many other trout mistakenly grab artificials also. A favorite technique is to cast a grasshopper imitation right to the streambank and then float/twitch it away, like a hopper that was blown into the drink and is trying to make it to shore.

Perhaps the best thing about cutts is the waters in which they are found—from mossy rain-forest streams of the Pacific Northwest to the mountain lakes and rivers of the Continental Divide. Their tendency to evolve into distinct strains when isolated by natural barriers makes them something of a "collector's trout," prized by fishermen who scorn the trout mass-produced by hatcheries.

But the cutt is a people's trout, too. Perhaps you, like me, are one of the millions of tourists who have hung over the railings of Fishing Bridge in Yellowstone National Park, admiring the sinuous trout swimming gracefully below. Those too are cutthroats.

If the brook trout has a serious rival for the title of Most Gorgeous, it is the **golden trout**, which originated in the Kern River system of California's Sierra Nevada range. Although the fish has been propagated by hatcheries and subsequently distributed throughout several Western states, it survives only in cold, high-altitude mountain lakes and streams. Reaching golden-trout waters usually means backpacking or horsepacking into a remote area and spending at least one night on the hard ground; for most of us, this only increases the allure of this striking and somewhat rare trout.

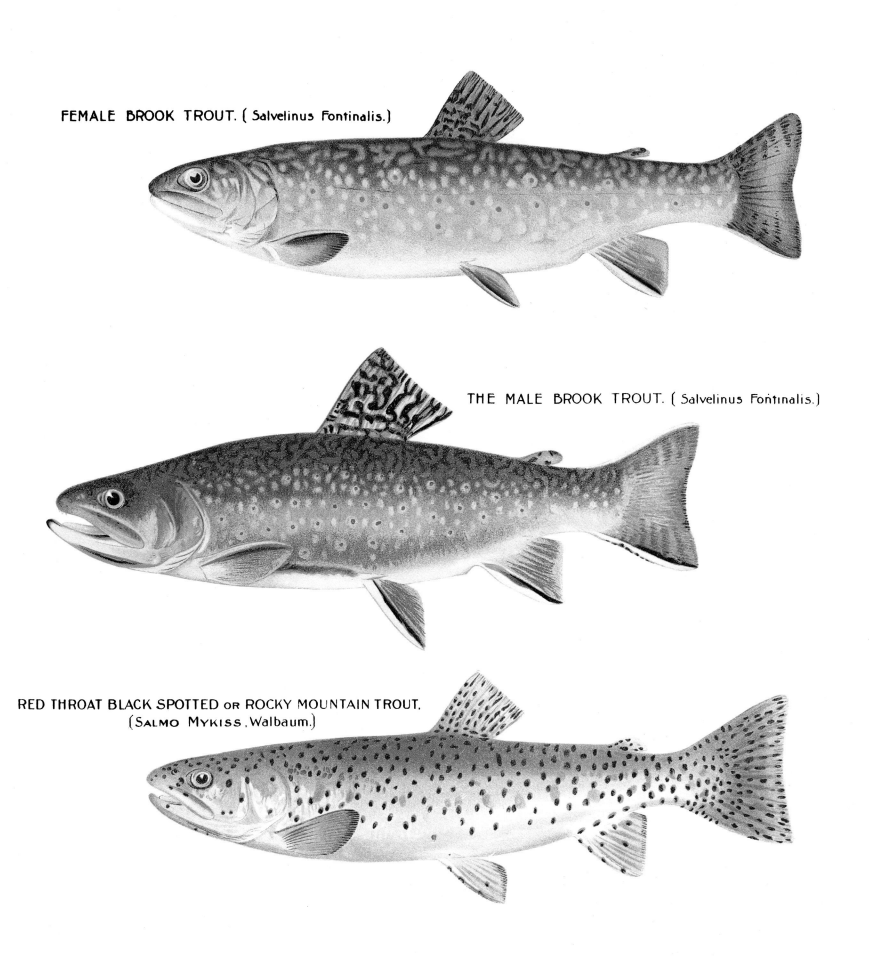

FEMALE BROOK TROUT. (Salvelinus Fontinalis.)

THE MALE BROOK TROUT. (Salvelinus Fontinalis.)

RED THROAT BLACK SPOTTED OR ROCKY MOUNTAIN TROUT.
(SALMO MYKISS, Walbaum.)

What the great lakes of the subarctic Canadian shield are famous for—giant lake trout. Northwest Territories photograph.

To describe the golden in words leaves the impression that this fish is a freak, a garish leftover from some genetic experiment. How else to explain a trout that looks like a conflagration of crimson, yellow, green, black and creamy white, all in shades that can only be described as *intense*? All combined with a heavily black-spotted tail and dorsal fin and a row of leftover parr markings, those vertical stripes that disappear from other trout as they mature. All I can tell you is that it works—the golden trout shimmers in the high-altitude sun in complete harmony with itself and its mountain environment. It's interesting to note that biologists who have raised goldens at lower altitudes find that the fish grows up a much more normal silvery-blue color.

The charrs are a genus of arctic salmonids that often cause considerable confusion among fishermen trying to keep scientific names, popular names and even appearances straight. But for our purposes they are simply trout—efficient predators, superb tackle-busters and thus great gamefish. And you don't need to travel to the far north to take charr, either; the eastern brook trout happens to be a charr, and so is the deep-dwelling lake trout.

Of all our salmonids, the **lake trout** is regularly surpassed in size only by the Pacific chinook (king) salmon. In the Great Lakes, where these trout were an important commercial fish before the lamprey plague drastically reduced the population, netters occasionally report lake trout of a hundred pounds or more, but a rod-and-reel fish of half that size is remarkable. Lake trout are widely distributed across almost all of Canada (where they're sometimes called gray trout), even well up into the Arctic islands, and from the Maritime coast west into Alaska to Bristol Bay (the local name is mackinaw). In the Lower 48, lake trout occur naturally only from northern New England (in Maine they're called togue) and upstate New York to the Great Lakes region. Lake trout have been transplanted, however, as far west and south as northern California.

Even more so than brookies, lakers demand cold water and they generally inhabit deep, clear, well-oxygenated lakes with good smelt populations. They are the premier gamefish of the tremendous lakes of the central Canadian shield—Great Bear, Great Slave, Athabaska and others—and anglers come from around the world to troll and cast for these huge wilderness lakers. In warmer climates, lake trout escape midsummer temperatures by living at depths of a hundred feet or more (sometimes much more), and about the only way to show them a lure is with deep-sinking leadcore line or even diving outriggers. Fish caught this way don't always put up much of a battle, but in colder waters or seasons—during the fall spawn, for example—when lake trout are often found in the shallows around rivermouths, they can be taken on lighter tackle. The main attraction of the laker, however, is always its size; they are usually two, three, maybe five times bigger than any other trout in their lakes, and older too.

Dolly Varden are western charr, found in great numbers especially in the streams of Alaska and the Northwest that Pacific salmon return to for spawning. Like the coastal rainbows, these Dollies feed voraciously on salmon eggs, and commercial fishermen claim they make a sizable dent in the salmon fingerling populations as well. This behavior—plus a certain natural boldness—has helped hatch the idea that Dolly Varden are freshwater sharks. Unfortunately, even dedicated catch-and-release sportsmen often regard Dollies as second-class citizens, treating them as "lunch fish." (As it happens, clean-water Dolly Varden taste wonderful, with a delicate flavor to their rosy pink meat. But perhaps anything cooked over an open fire on a streambank tastes better.)

But nevertheless they can be game fighters, and Dollies of ten pounds or more are common, at least in less-fished drainages. Dolly Varden like fast-flowing cold water. They're often caught in the shallow riffles below deeper pools, where the oxygen content is high and where anything (such as those salmon eggs) washing down from upstream is readily visible. They are often as gaudy as any trout, with white-edged fins, blazing orange-yellow bellies and white- or even lavender-spotted sides and bronze-green backs. The story goes that these fish are named after Dolly Varden, a character in Charles Dickens's *Barnaby Rudge* who supposedly also wore lavender spots. However, a friend who researched the matter claims that Dolly's dress is described only as cherry-colored; he thinks it more likely that—for example—a gold-rush miner

Happiness is almost twelve pounds of Alaskan Dolly Varden. Author's photograph.

Photographer Tim Leary captured the telltale "bloody" gill covers and lower jaw of the cutthroat trout.

Following spread:
A looking-glass view of a hooked Oregon cutthroat trout. Don Blegen photograph.

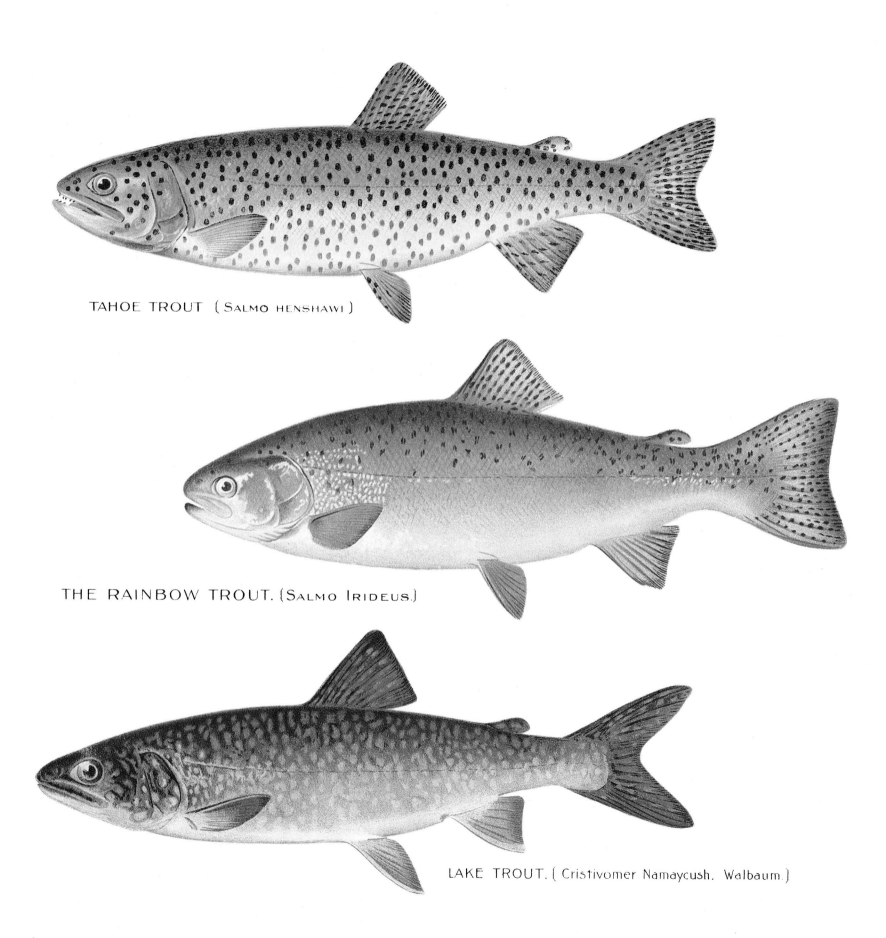

TAHOE TROUT (Salmo henshawi)

THE RAINBOW TROUT. (Salmo Irideus.)

LAKE TROUT. (Cristivomer Namaycush, Walbaum.)

THE BROWN TROUT. (Salmo Fario.)

who read Dickens evenings in his shack romantically named his claim "The Dolly Varden" (Dolly being a popular Victorian name). Then perhaps these fish were discovered in the stream nearby and picked up their name by association. . . . Well, it's a long shot. But no one's come up with a better explanation.

The **Arctic charr** is another coldwater northern salmonid, often similar enough in appearance to the Dolly Varden to cause confusion. In eastern Canada the fish is often found in brook trout water, and newcomers who see only the spectacularly colored bellies and fins of both fish find them hard to tell apart also. Arctic charr lack the worm-like black-on-green markings that brookies carry on their backs; and while charr may have no spots at all, the spots on any charr (brook trout included, remember) are light-colored while the spots of true trout are dark.

Distinguishing Arctics from Dollies is another matter. The rule of thumb is that if the spots on the fish are smaller than the iris of its eyes, then it's a Dolly Varden. However, as their ranges overlap only from central Canada westward, it's generally safe to say that an eastern charr—taken in Labrador, let's say, or Quebec, is indeed a charr and not a Dolly.

The charr is also a bold predator, often seemingly unafraid of man. Twice I've lost small grayling to charr that dashed out from the shadows to rip the fish off my hook. And a charr once bit me while I was squatting in the shallows, cleaning a grayling for the table. A gill raker was caught on my finger; I held my hand out into the current and tried to shake it away, and a six-pound charr rushed up and obligingly ripped it off. How do I know he was six pounds? While the fish hung in the current a yard out, chewing the morsel down and eyeing me hungrily, another fisherman extended his rod tip out over my head and dapped a streamer in front of the charr's nose. He took it unhesitatingly and shortly thereafter joined the grayling in the frying pan.

133

"A good gamefish is too valuable to be caught only once." This wild rainbow is receiving proper and careful handling as it is released; even the dog seems respectful. Author's photograph.

World Records

THE INTERNATIONAL GAME FISH Association, headquartered in Florida, is a nonprofit organization that has taken on the responsibility of vetting and keeping sportfishing records from around the world. It is also a powerful voice for fisheries conservation. It is not alone in the world in keeping such records, but it is the most respected of those groups, and it has officially designated representatives in virtually all the fishing corners of the world, no matter how remote. The records listed here are only for the fish mentioned in this book; the IGFA maintains data on many other species as well. For each fish there is an all-tackle record, which is the largest documented example of that species known to the IGFA; a group of line class records, that encompass fishing done with braided or monofilamentous lines (such as trolling, spincasting, baitfishing and so on); and then records for fish taken on fly tackle. Into which category a particular fish falls is determined by the breaking strain of the line or leader tippet it was caught on. The IGFA demands to see the actual line and hook a fish was taken with so that their lab may test it for actual tensile strength and also determine whether the rig meets their strict specifications for lengths, knots and so on.

The IGFA certification committee also naturally insists that record-contender fish be weighed on accurate scales. Most saltwater fishing marinas are equipped with such machinery. Anglers who fish in lakes and rivers, particularly in the bush where a government-certified grocery-story scale is not available nearby, may use handheld scales. But these must have been checked by the IGFA both before and after a fish is taken. The length and girth of a fish must also be recorded, and the IGFA wants to see photographs and the signatures of witnesses as well. If you're interested in competing for a spot in the record book, which is updated annually, contact the Association at 3000 East Las Olas Boulevard, Ft. Lauderdale, Florida 33316 for information. Many anglers carry with them a small kit of materials and information, as well as an entry form, to help them conform to the IGFA's requirements upon landing a large fish. It is no longer

necessary, in these enlightened times, to kill all but the largest trophy fish in order to qualify for a record.

The fly rod records only go up to the 8-kilogram, or 16-pound, tippet level because the fly line itself, above the tippet and the leader, has a breaking strain of approximately that itself, and so there is little point to fishing with a heavier tippet. This also explains why so many fly rod records, particularly in salt water, are substantially lower than line-class records—there is simply no way to boat a 500-pound tuna on a 16-pound leader tippet, barring incredible applications of time, money, perseverance and even more plain old luck.

Reading the records is not as dry as it might seem, for trends and imagined situations become obvious. Certain names pop up over and over—record hunters whose skill or motivation or personal wealth (or all three) let them pursue a dream all over North America or even the globe. It is still possible to identify certain species who are "underrecorded," where line classes are still vacant or the existing marks can easily be broken, especially if you know where in the world to go. Many fishermen plan their annual vacations around a trip to a certain lake or river or bay, where for a week or two they will singlemindedly try to better a certain mark. If they are successful, they change to another line or tippet class and go at it again. This was aided and abetted recently by one of the line manufacturers, who offered, for some years, $1,000 for each and every IGFA record set on their line. They never dreamed how successful this promotion would be, and ended up awarding more than $1 million to fishermen around the world. Some skillful and successful anglers earned very comfortable annual wages for several years simply by fishing hard (and smart) with Berkley Trilene.

Note that the largest examples of many species, particularly the freshwater and smaller saltwater fish, have been taken on middle-level line weights. This is partly because records are often simply a matter of luck, and partly because the great majority of non-record-hunting fishermen fish with mid-level tackle. They're not out to prove anything, just have a good time. Statisti-

cally, then, this large group has a better chance of striking gold. In many cases, as you progress to the heavier line classes, the size of the record actually diminishes. Often these fishermen are specifically looking for a record, and luck simply doesn't go their way—another manifestation of the old law that says the harder you try, the behinder you get. And only you can decide how glorious it is to hold the 12-pound record for bluegill sunfish. Many exceptions are found in the big-game species, the fish that approach the ton mark. It's difficult enough to boat such a creature on 130-pound line, and sizes usually increase with each line class.

No one will ever know how many record fish have been caught and not recorded—released unknowingly, or caught on tackle that doesn't meet IGFA specifications, or simply taken home and eaten! And many expert fishermen have caught record-breakers and chosen not to enter them to the IGFA—because of inconvenience or the desire not to kill or stress a fish or even because they simply don't want their name in print.

BASS Largemouth (*Micropterus salmoides*)
22 lbs 4 oz/10.09 kg   Montgomery Lake, Georgia 2 June 1932   George W. Perry
Line Class
1 kg (2 lb)   11 lbs/5.00 kg   Lake Casitas, California   25 May 1982   Frank Gasperov, Jr.
2 kg (4 lb)   14 lbs 4 oz/6.46 kg   Cachuma Lake, California   8 May 1985   Clint Johanson
4 kg (8 lb)   21 lbs 3 oz/9.61 kg   Oakview, California   4 March 1980   Raymond D. Easley
6 kg (12 lb)   18 lbs 8 oz/8.39 kg   Lake Isabella, California   6 January 1985   Chris Moore
8 kg (16 lb)   17 lbs 4 oz/7.82 kg   Polk County, Florida   6 July 1986   McArthur Bill O'Berry
10 kg (20 lb)   17 lbs 12 oz/8.05 kg   Lake Tohopekaliga, Florida   11 July 1986   John Q. Faircloth
Fly Rod - Tippet Class
1 kg (2 lb)   7 lbs 9 oz/3.43 kg   Arivaca lake, Arizona   17 March 1984   Corky Dufek
2 kg (4 lb)   6 lbs 7 oz/2.92 kg   Lake Tsala, Florida   15 June 1977   Terry G. Warson
4 kg (8 lb)   13 lbs 9 oz/6.15 kg   Lake Morena, California   4 April 1984   Ned S. Sewell
6 kg (12 lb)   12 lbs 9 oz/5.70 kg   Lake Tsala, Florida   25 March 1984   Robert M. Ekker
8 kg (16 lb)   11 lbs 2 oz/5.04 kg   Lake George, Florida   8 April 1978

BASS: Smallmouth (*Micropterus dolomieui*)
11 lbs 15 oz/5.41 kg   Dale Hollow Lake, Kentucky   9 July 1955   David L. Hayes
Line Class
1 kg (2 lb)   5 lbs 13 oz/2.63 kg   James River, Richmond, Virginia   20 March 1985   Robert H. Blevins

2 kg (4 lb)   6 lbs 13 oz/3.09 kg   Pickwick lake, Alabama   22 February 1983   Michael A. Curry
4 kg (8 lb)   10 lbs 8 oz/4.76 kg   Hendricks Creek, Kentucky   14 April 1986   Paul E. Beal
6 kg (12 lb)   8 lbs 8 oz/3.85 kg   Watts Bar Lake, Tennessee   6 April 1984   Lenny Cecil
8 kg (16 lb)   7 lbs 6 oz/3.34 kg   Tennessee River, Alabama   5 March 1986   Charles L. Tibbs

Fly Rod - Tippet Class
1 kg (2 lb)   2 lbs 3 oz/0.99 kg   George Lake, Manitoba, Canada   17 July 1983   James H. Miller
2 kg (4 lb)   4 lbs 1 oz/1.85 kg   Titus lake, New York   13 July 1985   Ronald D. Parl
4 kg (8 lb)   3 lbs 13 oz/1.72 kg   E. Grand Lake, N.B., Canada   16 May 1984   Bill White
4 kg (8 lb)   TIE   3 lbs 14 oz/1.78 kg   Ft. Loudon Lake, Tennessee   9 June 1984   Jean H. Leidersdorf
6 kg (12 lb)   4 lbs 6 oz/1.98 kg   James River, Virginia   4 September 1985   Noel Burkhead
8 kg (16 lb)   1 lb 9 ox/0.70 kg   Flaming Gorge Reservoir, Utah   20 September 1985   Ray Johnson

BASS: Striped, landlocked (*Morone saxatilis*) 59 lbs. 12 oz./27.10 kg.   Colorado River, Arizona   26 May 1977   Frank W. Smith
Line Class
1 kg (2 lb)   21 lbs 4 oz/9.63 kg   Savannah River, Georgia   15 July 1984   Stephen Bavazes
2 kg (4 lb)   38 lbs 12 oz/17.57 kg   Lake Norfork, Arkansas   9 February 1983   Bryce Frits, Jr.
4 kg (8 lb)   45 lbs 8 oz/20.63 kg   Lake Cumberland, Kentucky   18 April 1978   Walter C. Lilly
6 kg (12 lb)   47 lbs/21.31 kg   Flint River, Georgia   23 March 1983   Garry Whitehead
8 kg (16 lb)   59 lbs 12 oz/27.10 kg   Colorado River, Arizona   26 May 1977   Frank W. Smith
10 kg (20 lb)   52 lbs 8 oz/23.81 kg   Colorado River, Arizona   27 June 1976   Robert G. Stahl
15 kg (30 lb)   47 lbs 11 oz/21.64 kg   Flint River, Georgia   7 March 1986   Don Allen Fowler
24 kg (50 lb)   48 lbs 5 oz/21.91 kg   Flint River, Georgia   20 May 1983   John Hoffpauir, Jr.
Fly Rod - Tippet Class
1 kg (2 lb)   19 lbs 4 oz/8.73 kg   All American Canal, California   15 May 1982   Dr. Edward J. Cramer
2 kg (4 lb)   VACANT
4 kg (8 lb)   11 lbs 4 oz/5.10 kg   San Antonia Lake, California   18 October 1983   Roy Lawson
6 kg (12 lb)   9 lbs 8 oz/4.30 kg   Lake Havasu, California   15 July 1981   Paul lawson
8 kg (16 lb)   19 lbs 15 oz/9.06 kg   Silverwood lake, California   17 July 1986   Terry A. Baird
The four heavier classes appear to be ripe for the plucking—landlocked stripers grow to increasingly enormous sizes as their range widens (as the line class records indicate), and the relatively tiny fly rod marks likely indicate that the right angler has not yet found one of the monsters close enough to the surface for a good fly presentation. That day can't be far off, however.

BASS: White (*Morone chrysops*)   5 lbs 14 oz/2.66 kg   Kerr Lake, North Carolina   15 March 1986   Jim King
Line Class
1 kg (2 lb)   3 lbs 4 oz/1.47 kg   Devils Lake, North Dakota   29 December 1985   Matthew J. Cummings
2 kg (4 lb)   5 lbs 6 oz/2.43 kg   Grenada, Mississippi   21 April 1979   W.C. Mulvihill

4 kg (8 lb)   5 lbs 9 oz/2.52 kg   Colorado River, Texas   31 March 1977   David S. Cordill
6 kg (12 lb)   4 lbs 3 oz/1.89 kg   Frisco, Texas   24 February 1984   Geoff Cross
Fly Rod - Tippet Class
1 kg (2 lb)   2 lbs 9 oz/1.18 kg   Pomme de Terre River, Minnesota   20 May 1982   R.E. Massey
2 kg (4 lb)   2 lbs 9 oz/1.17 kg   Lake Nacimiento, California   12 March 1983   Butch Olson
4 kg (8 lb)   3 lbs 8 oz/1.58 kg   Nacimiento River, California   6 March 1981   Cory Wells
6 kg (12 lb)   VACANT
8 kg (16 lb)   VACANT

BLUEGILL: (*Lepomis macrochirus*)   4 lbs 12 oz/ 2.15 kg   Ketona Lake, Alabama   9 April 1950   T.S. Hudson
Line Class
1 kg (2 lb)   1 lb 8 oz/0.70 kg   Pine Mountain, Georgia   14 May 1986   Stephen King
2 kg (4 lb)   2 lbs 12 oz/1.24 kg   Vaughn, Michigan   30 June 1983   Gary Saylor
4 kg (8 lb)   1 lb 14 oz/0.86 kg   Page County, Iowa   12 May 1985   Will T. Knoll
6 kg (12 lb)   4 lbs 3 oz/1.89 kg   Hopkins County, Kentucky   5 August 1980   Phil M. Conyers
Fly Rod - Tppet Class
1 kg (2 lb)   1 lb 4 oz/0.56 kg   Glendale Reservoir, Idaho   9 August 1984   Jim Dougherty
2 kg (4 lb)   1 lb 13 oz/0.83 kg   Colorado Springs, Colorado   14 May 1986   Raymond C. Sapp
4 kg (8 lb)   2 lbs 12 oz/1.25 kg   Guilford County, North Carolina   4 November 1984   Curtis R. Holmes, Jr.
6 kg (12 lb)   VACANT
8 kg (16 lb)   VACANT

BULLHEAD: black (*Ictalurus melas*)   8 lbs/ 3.62 kg   Lake Waccabuc, New York   1 August 1951   Kani Evans
Line Class
1 kg (2 lb)   2 lbs 13 oz/1.28 kg   Washington, Iowa   26 May 1985   Richard Greiner
2 kg (4 lb)   1 lb 15 oz/0.87 kg   Andrew County, Missouri   31 March 1984   Larry Lowdon
4 kg (8 lb)   6 lbs 9 oz/2.99 kg   Cowley County, Kansas   14 April 1985   Lyle J. Houghton
6 kg (12 lb)   7 lbs 5 oz/3.32 kg   Havana, Kansas   13 May 1985   David A. Tremain
Fly Rod - Tippet Class
All fly rod classes are VACANT

BULLHEAD: brown (*Ictalurus nebulosus*)   5 lbs 8 oz/2.49 kg   Veal Pond, Georgia   22 May 1975   Jimmy Andrews
Line Class
1 kg (2 lb)   2 lbs 4 oz/1.03 kg   Lake Beauclaire, Florida   15 January 1986   Roger Meyer
2 kg (4 lb)   2 lbs 14 oz/1.32 kg   Mountain Creek Lake, Georgia   26 February 1985   Stephen King
4 kg (8 lb)   3 lbs 13 oz/1.74 kg   Montgomery County, Alabama   8 April 1984   Charles A. Lane
6 kg (12 lb)   5 lbs 8 oz/2.49 kg   Veal Pond, Georgia   22 May 1975   Jimmy Andrews
Fly Rod - Tippet Class
All fly rod classes are VACANT

CATFISH: blue (*Ictalurus furcatus*)   97 lbs/ 43.99 kg   Missouri River. South Dakota   16 September 1959   Edward B. Elliott
Line Class
1 kg (2 lb)   4 lbs/1.81 kg   Kinston, North Carolina   7 July 1984   Debra Kay Crews
2 kg (4 lb)   27 lbs 1 oz/12.21 kg   Haakon County Lakes, South Dakota   29 April 1976   O.R. (Bob) Brancel
4 kg (8 lb)   58 lbs 8 oz/26.53 kg   Irvine Lake, California   6 July 1986   Glenn E. Bell

6 kg (12 lb)   67 lbs 14 oz/30.79 kg   Lake Texoma, Texas   12 November 1985   Nonnie Ledbetter
8 kg (16 lb)   81 lbs/36.74 kg   Kentucky Lake, Kentucky   22 June 1986   Dana A. Ballard
10 kg (20 lb)   79 lbs/35.83 kg   Lake Texoma, Oklahoma   14 May 1984   Viola McNabb
15 kg (30 lb)   81 lbs/36.74 kg   Washita River, Oklahoma   19 July 1985   Jerry G. Buchanan
24 kg (50 lb)   69 lbs/31.29 kg   Lake Texoma, Oklahoma   28 November 1980   W.H. Kirk
37 kg (80 lb)   80 lbs/36.28 kg   Lake Texoma, Oklahoma   28 November 1980   Ron J. Smith
60 kg (130 lb)   12 lbs 9 oz/5.69 kg   Kentucky Dam, Tennessee   19 June 1985   Teddy R. Coleman
Fly Rod - Tippet Class
All fly rod classes are VACANT

CATFISH: channel (*Ictalurus punctatus*)   58 lbs/26.30 kg   Santee-Cooper Reservoir, South Carolina   7 July 1964   W.B. Whaley
Line Class
1 kg (2 lb)   20 lbs 6 oz/9.27 kg   Red River, Manitoba   28 August 1985   Jeff C. Suggitt
2 kg (4 lb)   22 lbs 1 oz/10 kg   Red River, Manitoba   30 June 1986   Lamont M. Wegner
4 kg (8 lb)   37 lbs 6 oz/16.95 kg   Sebastian River, Florida   16 January 1983   Max D. Nowotne
6 kg (12 lb)   32 lbs 3 oz/14.61 kg   Satilla River, Georgia   30 October 1977   James I. Lentz
8 kg (16 lb)   41 lbs 8 oz/18.82 kg   Snake River, Nebraska   26 July 1985   Johnnie F. Cunning
10 kg (20 lb)   41 lbs/18.59 kg   Dunlap, Tennessee   30 July 1982   Clint Walters, Jr.
15 kg (30 lb)   41 lbs 8 oz/18.82 kg   Snake River, Nebraska   11 August 1986   Heather Jo Cunning
24 kg (50 lb)   33 lbs/14.96 kg   Snake River, Nebraska   15 August 1986   Johnnie F. Cunning
37 kg (80 lb)   25 lbs 2 oz/11.39 kg   Red River, Manitoba   2 August 1986   Rodney D. Adams
Fly Rod - Tippet Class
1 kg (2 lb)   1 lb 3 oz/0.54 kg   Coosa County, Alabama   28 June 1986   Vance H. Baker
2 kg (4 lb)   7 lbs/3.17 kg   Kinston, North Carolina   21 May 1984   Thomas E. Crews
4 kg (8 lb)   1 lb 1 oz/0.49 kg   Goose Creek, Virginia   6 August 1983   Rochlyn L. Lorey, Sr.
6 kg (12 lb)   2 lbs 15 oz/1.34 kg   Coosa County, Alabama   30 June 1986   Vance H. Baker
8 kg (16 lb)   9 lbs/4.08 kg   Lake Washington, Florida   15 March 1985   Robert C. Newby

CATFISH: flathead (*Ictalurus olivaris*)   98 lbs/ 44.45 kg   Lewisville, Texas   2 June 1986   William O. Stephens
Line Class
1 kg (2 lb)   30 lbs 1 oz/13.63 kg   St. Croix River, Minnesota   8 August 1986   Floyd F. Michlitsch
2 kg (4 lb)   49 lbs 8 oz/22.45 kg   Grays Lake, Iowa   1 July 1986   Pat Brady
4 kg (8 lb)   54 lbs/24.49 kg   Watts Bar Lake, Tennessee   30 June 1984   Eddie L. Rogers
4 kg (8 lb)   Tie   54 lbs/24.49 kg   Francis Case Reservoir, South Dakota   4 July 1986   Martin K. Horley
6 kg (12 lb)   91 lbs 4 oz/41.39 kg   Lake Lewisville, Texas   28 March 1984   Mike Rogers
8 kg (16 lb)   55 lbs/24.94 kg   thomas Hill Lake, Missouri   26 April 1986   Mark Lynn Epperson
10 kg (20 lb)   64 lbs 2 oz/29.08 kg   St. Croix River, Wisconsin   20 August 1985   Dave Olson
15 kg (30 lb)   98 lbs/44.45 kg   Lewisville, Texas   2 June 1986   William O. Stephens
24 kg (50 lb)   57 lbs 4 oz/25.96 kg   Colorado River, Arizona   16 April 1985   Mike Hughes
37 kg (80 lb)   34 lbs 8 oz/15.64 kg   St. Croix

River, Minnesota 22 August 1985 Joel M. Anderson
60 kg (130 lb) 41 lbs 7 oz/18.79 kg St. Croix River, Minnesota 2 September 1985 Floyd F. Michlitsch
Fly Rod - Tippet Class
All fly rod classes are VACANT

CHAR: arctic (*Salvelinus alpinus*) 32 lbs 9 oz/ 14.77 kg Tree River, Northwest Territories 30 July 1981 Jeffery L. Ward
Line Class
1 kg (2 lb) 17 lbs 4 oz/7.82 kg Kugaryak River, Northwest Territories 26 August 1981 Raymond Goodrich
2 kg (4 lb) 21 lbs/9.52 kg Kugaryuk River, Northwest Territories 26 August 1981 Raymond Goodrich
4 kg (8 lb) 22 lbs 8 oz/10.20 kg Kugaryuk River, Northwest Territories 28 August 1978 Ruby A. Goodrich
6 kg (12 lb) 25 lbs/11.34 kg Kugaryuk River, Northwest Territories 28 August 1978 Raymond Goodrich
8 kg (16 lb) 28 lbs/12.70 kg Tree River, Northwest Territories 21 August 1985 Robert J. Frost, MD
10 kg (20 lb) 24 lbs/10.88 kg Victoria Island, Northwest Territories 30 July 1985 Chuck McCauley
15 kg (30 lb) 21 lbs 8 oz/9.75 kg Victoria Island, Northwest Territories 1 August 1981 Robert W. Kitchen
Fly Rod - Tippet Class
1 kg (2 lb) 6 lbs 12 oz/3.06 kg Basset Brook, Labrador 1 September 1983 Franklin F. Webb
2 kg (4 lb) 11 lbs/4.98 kg Coppermine River, Northwest Territories 4 July 1985 Thomas M. Bruno
4 kg (8 lb) 18 lbs 2 oz/8.22 kg Victoria Island, Northwest Territories 25 July 1981 Elmer M. Rusten
6 kg (12 lb) 15 lbs/6.80 kg Victoria Island, Northwest Territories 2 September 1980 Elmer M. Rusten
8 kg (16 lb) 14 lbs 12 oz/6.69 kg Kugaryuak River, Northwest Territories 14 August 1984 Jim Dixon

CRAPPIE: black (*Pomoxis nigromaculatus*) 4 lbs 8 oz/2.05 kg Kerr Lake, Virginia 1 March 1981 L. Carl Herring, Jr.
Line Class
1 kg (2 lb) 3 lbs 2 oz/1.44 kg Chickahominy Lake, Virginia 10 August 1986 Max Tongier, Jr.
2 kg (4 lb) 4 lbs 4 oz/1.92 kg Beaver Dam Lake, North Carolina 25 March 1984 Chris Ransom
4 kg (8 lb) 4 lbs 8 oz/2.05 kg Kerr Lake, Virginia 1 March 1981 L. Carl Herring, Jr.
6 kg (12 lb) 4 lbs 4 oz/1.92 kg Paint Creek, Alabama 18 March 1984 Sherril S. Harris
Fly Rod - Tippet Class
1 kg (2 lb) 2 lbs 3 oz/1.01 kg Lee Hall Reservoir, Virginia 20 March 1985 Max Tongier
2 kg (4 lb) 1 lb 9 oz/0.73 kg Carlisle County, Kentucky 11 May 1986 Allen Beard
4 kg (8 lb) 2 lbs 6 oz/1.07 kg Lee Hall Reservoir, Virginia 21 March 1985 Max Tongier
6 kg (12 lb) VACANT
8 kg (16 lb) VACANT

CRAPPIE: white (*Pomoxis annularis*) 5 lbs 3 oz/ 2.35 kg Enid Dam, Mississippi 31 July 1957 Fred L. Bright
Line Class
1 kg (2 lb) 2 lbs 11 oz/1.21 kg Delaware River, Pennsylvania 3 May 1986 Patricia Phillips
1 kg (2 lb) Tie 2 lbs 11 oz/1.21 kg Beaver Dam Lake, North Carolina 25 March 1984

Chris Ransom
2 kg (4 lb) 3 lbs/1.36 kg Delaware River, Pennsylvania 21 April 1985 John J. Phillips, Jr.
4 kg (8 lb) 3 lbs 12 oz/1.70 kg Alabama River, Alabama 31 March 1982 James E. Black
6 kg (12 lb) 4 lbs/1.81 kg Rome, Georgia 19 March 1980 Ken Wright
Fly Rod - Tippet Class
2 kg (4 lb) 2 lbs 8 oz/1.13 kg Amelia County, Virginia 6 September 1986 Adam S. Plotkin
All other fly rod classes are VACANT

DOLLY VARDEN: (*Salvelinus malma*) 10 lbs 2 oz/ 4.59 kg Kenai River, Alaska 31 August 1986 Ronald G. Reeves, Jr.
Line Class
1 kg (2 lb) 4 lbs 9 oz/2.09 kg Quigmy River, Alaska 5 July 1986 Terry Chase
2 kg (4 lb) 5 lbs 12 oz/2.62 kg Rocky River, Alaska 14 July 1986 Martin Vanderploeg
4 kg (8 lb) 8 lbs 1 oz/3.66 kg Nakwasina River, Alaska 14 July 1985 Loyal J. Johnson
6 kg (12 lb) 10 lbs 2 oz/4.59 kg Kenai River, Alaska 31 August 1986 Ronald G. Reeves, Jr.
Fly Rod - Tippet Class
1 kg (2 lb) 4 lbs 12 oz/2.15 kg Painter Creek, Alaska 23 September 1985 Burton R. Leed
2 kg (4 lb) 5 lbs 4 oz/2.38 kg Painter Creek, Alaska 27 September 1985 Burton R. Leed
4 kg (8 lb) 4 lbs 8 oz/2.04 kg Painter Creek, Alaska 24 September 1985 Burton R. Leed
6 kg (12 lb) 8 lbs/3.62 kg Painter Creek, Alaska 24 September 1985 Burton R. Leed
8 kg (16 lb) 5 lbs/2.26 kg Togiak, Alaska 10 September 1985 Robert L. Andreae
This is a good example of the results of a determined effort upon a previously vacant set of tippet classes—one angler, well prepared with certified scales, proper tippets, witnesses, camera, measuring tape and IGFA forms, in one week's fishing on one river, achieved almost a clean sweep. Now the job is to knock him off, in friendly fashion, of course.

GRAYLING: arctic (*Thymallus arcticus*) 5 lbs 15 oz/2.69 kg Katseyedie River, Northwest Territories 16 August 1967 Jeanne P. Branson
Line Class
1 kg (2 lb) 3 lbs 1 oz/1.38 kg Great Bear Lake, Northwest Territories 17 August 1983 Joseph B. Doggett
2 kg (4 lb) 4 lbs 10 oz/2.09 kg Great Bear Lake, Northwest Territories 9 August 1984 Carol P. Bull
4 kg (8 lb) 5 lbs 4 oz/2.38 kg Great Bear Lake, Northwest Territories 1 August 1986 Silvio Ronconi
6 kg (12 lb) 4 lbs 4 oz/1.92 kg Port Radium, Northwest Territories 21 August 1978 Raymond Goodrich
8 kg (16 lb) 3 lbs 5 oz/1.50 kg Casa-de-Paga River, Alaska 25 September 1985 M. Shane Kirkland
10 kg (20 lb) 3 lbs 7 oz/1.55 kg Casa-de-Paga River, Alaska 25 September 1985 Jack P. Kirkland
Fly Rod - Tippet Class
1 kg (2 lb) 3 lbs 8 oz/1.60 kg Great Slave lake, Northwest Territories 6 September 1984 Don L. Guhlke
2 kg (4 lb) 3 lbs 8 oz/1.58 kg Great Bear Lake, Northwest Territories 18 August 1983 Joseph B. Doggett
4 kg (8 lb) 3 lbs 8 oz/1.58 kg Kasba Lake, Manitoba 10 August 1982 Ian P. MacDougall
6 kg (12 lb) 3 lbs 3 oz/1.46 kg Ugashik River, Alaska 9 July 1985 Jim Teeny

6 kg (12 lb) TIE 3 lbs 4 oz/1.48 kg Ugashik River, Alaska 30 July 1985 Danielle Smith
8 kg (16 lb) 2 lbs 12 oz/1.24 kg Stark River, Northwest Territories 13 July 1984 Bud F. Garland

MUSKELLUNGE: (*Esox masquinongy*) 69 lbs 15 oz/ 31.72 kg St. Lawrence River, New York 22 September 1957 Arthur Lawton
Line Class
1 kg (2 lb) 6 lbs 3 oz/2.80 kg Lake Kishkutena, Ontario 16 August 1986 Michael J. Baranowski
2 kg (4 lb) 35 lbs 8 oz/16.10 kg Leech Lake, Minnesota 24 May 1980 Bill Golembeck
4 kg (8 lb) 39 lbs 2 oz/17.74 kg Allegheny River, New York 19 November 1982 Gary Donahue
6 kg (12 lb) 50 lbs/22.67 kg Lake Nosbonsing, Ontario 21 September 1983 Terry L. Bachman
8 kg (16 lb) 45 lbs/20.42 kg 1,000 Island lake, Michigan 26 July 1980 Dr. William H. Pivar
10 kg (20 lb) 48 lbs 9 oz/22.02 kg Pewaukee Lake, Wisconsin 19 November 1977 Joe Ehrhardt
15 kg (30 lb) 56 lbs 7 oz/25.59 kg Manitou Lake, Ontario 30 August 1984 Gene Borucki
24 kg (50 lb) 55 lbs/24.94 kg Moon River, Ontario 11 October 1981 Gary Ishii
37 kg (80 lb) 35 lbs/15.87 kg Lake of the Woods, Ontario 2 November 1985 Richard Zebleckis
Fly Rod - Tippet Class
All fly rod classes are VACANT

MUSKELLUNGE: tiger (*E. masquinongy x Esox Lucius*) 51 lbs 3 oz/23.21 kg Lac Vieux-Desert, Wisconsin/ Michigan 16 July 1919 John A. Knobla
Line Class
1 kg (2 lb) VACANT
2 kg (4 lb) 18 lbs 8 oz/8.39 kg Stevenson Dam, Pennsylvania 5 July 1983 Samuel Brisini, Jr.
4 kg (8 lb) 30 lbs 8 oz/13.83 kg Round Lake, Wisconsin 12 May 1976 Leonard S. Grunow
6 kg (12 lb) 25 lbs 12 oz/11.67 kg Lac Vieux Desert, Wisconsin 2 October 1981 Dave Gallagher
8 kg (16 lb) 23 lbs 15 oz/10.85 kg Lake James, North Carolina 17 October 1983 John Ray Effler
10 kg (20 lb) 31 lbs 14 oz/14.45 kg St. Lawrence River, New York 1 October 1979 George C. Pifer
15 kg (30 lb) 31 lbs 8 oz/14.28 kg White Sand Lake, Wisconsin 25 August 1983 Matthew C. Belan
24 kg (50 lb) 28 lbs/12.70 kg Eagle Lake, Ontario 2 August 1982 Mark A. Wright
Fly Rod - Tippet Class
4 kg (8 lb) 17 lbs 4 oz/7.82 kg Freehold, New York 29 July 1983 Paul A. Schmookler
6 kg (12 lb) 30 lbs 6 oz/13.80 kg St. Lawrence River, Quebec 20 October 1985 Michel D. Croteau
All other fly rod classes are VACANT

PERCH: white (*Morone americana*) 4 lbs 12 oz/ 2.15 kg Messalonskee Lake, Maine 4 June 1949 Mrs. Earl Small
Line Class
1 kg (2 lb) 2 lbs 8 oz/1.13 kg West Kingston, Rhode Island 28 September 1982 Albert S. Ferris
2 kg (4 lb) 2 lbs 4 oz/1.02 kg Nantucket Island, Massachusetts 18 November 1985 William M. Pew
4 kg (8 lb) 2 lbs 8 oz/1.13 kg Coonamessett Pond, Massachusetts 29 June 1985 Chris Salpoglou

6 kg (12 lb) 2 lbs 6 oz/1.07 kg West Kingston, Rhode Island 25 September 1982 Frances E. Ferris
Fly Rod - Tippet Class
All fly rod classes are VACANT

PERCH: yellow (*Perca flavescens*) 4 lbs 3 oz/1.91 kg Bordentown, New Jersey May 1865 Dr. C.C. Abbot
Line Class
1 kg (2 lb) 2 lbs 9 oz/1.18 kg Yuba Reservoir, Utah 5 July 1984 Ray Johnson
2 kg (4 lb) 2 lbs 11 oz/1.23 kg Yuba Reservoir, Utah 4 July 1984 Ray Johnson
4 kg (8 lb) 2 lbs 5 oz/1.05 kg Yuba Reservoir, Utah 4 July 1984 Ray Johnson
6 kg (12 lb) 1 lb 15 oz/0.87 kg Barbers Pond, Rhode Island 26 September 1986 Holly Kristen Ferris
Fly Rod - Tippet Class
6 kg (12 lb) 1 lb 4 oz/0.56 kg Pakwash Lake, Ontario 16 October 1985 Lawrence E. Hudnall
All other fly rod classes are VACANT

PICKEREL: chain (*Esox niger*) 9 lbs 6 oz/4.25 kg Homerville, Georgia 17 February 1961 Baxley McCuaig, Jr.
Line Class
1 kg (2 lb) 5 lbs 2 oz/2.32 kg Newport News, Virginia 16 October 1983 Max Tongier, Jr.
2 kg (4 lb) 5 lbs 11 oz/2.57 kg Schoolhouse Pond, Rhode Island 11 August 1981 Albert S. Ferris
4 kg (8 lb) 6 lbs 11 oz/3.03 kg Richmond, Rhode Island 13 April 1985 David A. Greene
6 kg (12 lb) 6 lbs 14 oz/3.11 kg Lee Hall Reservoir, Virginia 3 January 1982 Max Tongier, Jr.
Fly Rod - Tippet Class
1 kg (2 lb) 3 lbs 5 oz/1.52 kg Newport News, Virginia 12 April 1984 Max Tongier, Jr.
2 kg (4 lb) 4 lbs 4 oz/1.92 kg Lovell's Pond, Massachusetts 24 October 1985 Jeffrey Joiner
4 kg (8 lb) 2 lbs 14 oz/1.30 kg Newport News, Virginia 12 April 1984 Max Tongier, Jr.
All other fly rod classes are VACANT

PIKE: northern (*Esox lucius*) 46 lbs 2 oz/20.92 kg Sacandaga Reservoir, New York 15 September 1940 Peter Dubuc
Line Class
1 kg (2 lb) 23 lbs 4 oz/10.54 kg Great Horden Lake, Kentucky 8 January 1984 John Pearn
2 kg (4 lb) 24 lbs 2 oz/10.96 kg Furusund, Sweden 25 May 1986 Yngre Pettersson
4 kg (8 lb) 35 lbs 8 oz/16.10 kg Lake Frigon, Quebec 26 June 1984 Thomas N. Quinzi
6 kg (12 lb) 34 lbs 6 oz/15.62 kg Angso, Sweden 2 May 1983 Magnus Herou
8 kg (16 lb) 27 lbs 8 oz/12.50 kg Moon Lake, Quebec 20 October 1986 Vince MacDonell
10 kg (20 lb) 29 lbs/13.15 kg Colin Lake, Alberta 20 September 1985 David H. Tenney
15 kg (30 lb) 31 lbs/14.06 kg Black Lake, Saskatchewan 9 June 1986 Alan L. Grove
24 kg (50 lb) 30 lbs/13.60 kg Trosa, Sweden 2 May 1986 Bill Tenney
As a highly desirable and world-ranging gamefish, the northern pike's records show a classic leveling-off of size as line weights increase. The all-tackle record seems suspect today, being not only fully 12 pounds greater than anything else listed but also close to 50 years old. Yet pike of that size and even slightly larger are caught every year now in northern Europe and occasionally in the British Isles; they simply are not listed with the IGFA, perhaps because of certification problems.
Fly Rod - Tippet Class
1 kg (2 lb) 24 lbs 3 oz/10.97 kg Brabant Is-

land, Northwest Territories 31 July 1985 John A. Propp
2 kg (4 lb) 22 lbs 8 oz/10.20 kg MacKenzie River, Northwest Territories 27 July 1983 John A. Propp
4 kg (8 lb) 21 lbs 8 oz/9.75 kg Great Slave Lake, Northwest Territories 13 August 1981 John A. Propp
6 kg (12 lb) 17 lbs 8 oz/7.95 kg Great Slave Lake, Northwest Territories 18 July 1983 Mickey Anderson
8 kg (16 lb) 22 lbs/9.97 kg MacKenzie River, Northwest Territories 5 August 1980 Charles A. Resen

SALMON: Atlantic (*Salmo salar*) 79 lbs 2 oz/35.89 kg Tana River, Norway 1928 Henrik Henriksen
Line Class
1 kg (2 lb) 4 lbs 11 oz/2.15 kg Ausable River, New York 20 September 1986 Edward T. Monsoor II
2 kg (4 lb) 16 lbs/7.25 kg Lac Tremblant, Quebec 19 May 1984 Pierre Lefebvre
4 kg (8 lb) 25 lbs 13 oz/11.73 kg River Morrum, Sweden 22 May 1983 Bjarke Schmidt
6 kg (12 lb) 33 lbs 15 oz/15.40 kg River Namsen, Norway 7 June 1984 Rolf Hagstrom
8 kg (16 lb) 38 lbs 9 oz/17.50 kg River Namsen, Norway 3 June 1981 Borge M. Jensen
10 kg (20 lb) 40 lbs 1 oz/18.20 kg River Namsen, Norway 2 July 1984 Inge M. Storm
15 kg (30 lb) 30 lbs 2 oz/13.67 kg River Gaula, Norway 15 July 1986 Hakan Brugard
24 kg (50 lb) 4 lbs 12 oz/2.15 kg George River, Quebec 20 August 1984 Jack Fallon
Why did Jack Fallon, a highly experienced and world-traveling fisherman, choose to set a "world record" with a fish not even 10 percent of the weight of his line class? Not much glory there, surely, yet only he knows for sure. The outfitter who guided him on the George may have insisted upon it, as a way of getting his operation listed with the IGFA. Atlantic salmon records in North America are necessarily slanted towards the fly rod category because salmon may legally be caught only on flies. In Europe, any tackle goes, hence the larger Scandinavian fish in the freshwater section, most of which were taken on prawns (large shrimp) lashed to bait hooks and cast with spinning tackle.
Fly Rod - Tippet Class
1 kg (2 lb) 22 lbs/9.97 kg Alta River, Norway 28 June 1983 Darryl G. Behrman
2 kg (4 lb) 29 lbs/17.46 kg Alta River, Norway 30 June 1983 Darryl G. Behrman
4 kg (8 lb) 31 lbs 8 oz/14.28 kg Alta River, Norway 25 June 1983 Darryl G. Behrman
6 kg (12 lb) 44 lbs 12 oz/20.29 kg Moisie River, Quebec 4 June 1980 Leopold Miousse
8 kg (16 lb) 47 lbs/21.31 kg Cascapedia River, Quebec 16 June 1982 Donal C. O'Brien, Jr.
Atlantic salmon have traditionally been an upper-class fish, especially in Europe, where the aristocrats fished for them with flies almost exclusively, and there is a strong tradition of salmon fishing that goes back more than a century. Today's modern records, which date from the inception of IGFA's data-keeping, don't take into account the dozens—perhaps hundreds—of well-documented European salmon of 60, 70 and even 90 pounds that were taken before the 1960s.

SALMON: king (*Oncorhynchus tshawytscha*) 97 lbs 4 oz/44.11 kg Kenai River, Alaska 17 May 1985 Les Anderson
Line Class
1 kg (2 lb) 34 lbs 10 oz/15.70 kg Chuitt River, Alaska 6 July 1984 Robert E. Hamilton
2 kg (4 lb) 39 lbs 12 oz/18.11 kg Kenai River,

Alaska 31 May 1984 Craig S. Archer
4 kg (8 lb) 62 lbs 4 oz/28.23 kg Kenai River, Alaska 31 July 1984 Donald R. Cloyd
6 kg (12 lb) 67 lbs 4 oz/30.50 kg Kenai River, Alaska 31 July 1986 Michael J. Fenton
8 kg (16 lb) 77 lbs 8 oz/35.15 kg Kenai River, Alaska 18 July 1985 Jerry Downey
10 kg (20 lb) 84 lbs 4 oz/38.21 kg Cook Inlet, Alaska 14 July 1984 Ray Holten
15 kg (30 lb) 97 lbs 4 oz/44.11 kg Kenai River, Alaska 17 May 1985 Les Anderson
24 kg (50 lb) 81 lbs 4 oz/36.85 kg Deep Creek, Alaska 15 July 1985 Dale C. Anderson
37 kg (80 lb) 65 lbs/29.48 kg Kenai River, Alaska 24 July 1986 Max Pruett, Jr.
60 kg (130 lb) 45 lbs/20.41 kg Kenai River, Alaska 26 June 1986 Kristian Iverson
Why does the Kenai River hold so many king (and other Pacific) salmon records? The main reason of course is that it is one of the world's prime king rivers. Another, equally important, however, is that part of the Kenai water is accessible by road from Anchorage—highly unusual, as most of Alaska is bush and so out of reach of those who cannot fly in—and so the fishing pressure is enormous. Many fish plus many fishermen equals records.
Fly Rod - Tippet Class
1 kg (2 lb) 22 lbs 4 oz/10.09 kg Little Manistee, Michigan 29 August 1983 Kenneth R. Darwin
2 kg (4 lb) 29 lbs/13.15 kg Karluk River, Alaska 11 July 1984 Rod Neubert, D.V.M.
4 kg (8 lb) 52 lbs 8 oz/23.81 kg Chetco River, Oregon 10 November 1982 Bob Byers
6 kg (12 lb) 44 lbs 6 oz/20.13 kg Chetco River, Oregon 4 November 1982 Patt Wardlaw
8 kg (16 lb) 54 lbs 8 oz/24.72 kg Chetco River, oregon 24 October 1981 Ed Given

SALMON: chum (*Oncorhynchus keta*) 32 lbs/14.51 kg Behm Canal, Alaska 7 June 1985 Fredrick E. Thynes
Line Class
1 kg (2 lb) 15 lbs 7 oz/7.00 kg Fish Creek, Alaska 1 August 1986 Jeff Trom
2 kg (4 lb) 17 lbs 5 oz/7.85 kg Fish Creek, Alaska 1 August 1986 Martin Vanderploeg
4 kg (8 lb) 15 lbs 6 oz/6.97 kg Fish Creek, Alaska 1 August 1986 Jeff Trom
6 kg (12 lb) 18 lbs 8 oz/8.40 kg Kilchis River, Oregon 12 December 1984 Richard A. Weber
8 kg (16 lb) 22 lbs 2 oz/10.03 kg Hakai Pass, British Columbia 23 June 1985 Scott Bergey
10 kg (20 lb) 25 lbs 2 oz/11.40 kg Ketchikan, Alaska 1 July 1985 Tracy McLean
15 kg (30 lb) 17 lbs 5 oz/7.86 kg Kilchis River, Oregon 21 November 1985 Richard A. Weber
Fly Rod - Tippet Class
1 kg (2 lb) 13 lbs/5.89 kg Pah River, Alaska 18 August 1986 Lawrence E. Hudnall
2 kg (4 lb) 12 lbs 11 oz/5.75 kg Alagnak River, Alaska 17 July 1983 Gary Hibler
4 kg (8 lb) 23 lbs 4 oz/10.54 kg Dean River Channel, British Columbia 19 August 1983 Rod Neubert, D.V.M.
6 kg (12 lb) 23 lbs 14 oz/10.82 kg Stillaguamish River, Washington 7 December 1985 Michael F. Graham
8 kg (16 lb) 21 lbs 2 oz/9.60 kg Kilchis River, Oregon 18 November 1984 Jimbo Fowler

SALMON: silver (*Oncorhynchus kisutch*) 31 lbs/14.06 kg Cowichan Bay, BC 11 October 1947 Mrs. Lee Halberg
Line Class
1 kg (2 lb) 15 lbs 4 oz/6.91 kg Juneau, Alaska 16 August 1986 Harvey Minatoya, MD
2 kg (4 lb) 15 lbs 15 oz/7.24 kg Kenai River, Alaska 4 September 1985 Pat K. Johnson

4 kg (8 lb) 19 lbs 8 oz/8.84 kg Situk River, Alaska 20 September 1984 Melvin E. Snook
6 kg (12 lb) 21 lbs 8 oz/9.75 kg Prince William Sound, Alaska 18 August 1984 Robert Dolphin, DVM
8 kg (16 lb) 20 lbs 8 oz/9.29 kg Kenai River, Alaska 24 September 1984 Carloss R. Kirkman
10 kg (20 lb) 30 lbs 12 oz/13.94 kg Salmon River, New York 12 September 1985 Bub Cornish
15 kg (30 lb) 24 lbs 10 oz/11.16 kg Lake Ontario, New York 7 September 1984 Tom Cornell
24 kg (50 lb) 17 lbs 4 oz/7.82 kg Kenai River, Alaska 14 September 1984 Paul W. Pearson
Fly Rod - Tippet Class
1 kg (2 lb) 12 lbs/5.44 kg Karluk River, Alaska 10 September 1982 Ken Hower, Jr.
2 kg (4 lb) 15 lbs 8 oz/7.03 kg Karluk River, Alaska 9 October 1981 Rod Neubert, D.V.M.
4 kg (8 lb) 17 lbs 8 oz/7.93 kg Karluk Lake, Alaska 11 October 1981 Rod Neubert, D.V.M.
6 kg (12 lb) 19 lbs/8.61 kg Karluk Lake, Alaska 20 September 1983 Kevin Becker
8 kg (16 lb) 12 lbs 4 oz/5.55 kg Togiak, Alaska 9 September 1985 Robert L. Andreae

SALMON: pink (*Oncorhynchus gorbuscha*)
12 lbs 9 oz/5.69 kg Moose & Kenai Rivers, Alaska 17 August 1974 Steven Alan Lee
Line Class
1 kg (2 lb) 10 lbs 4 oz/4.64 kg Karluk River, Alaska 13 July 1984 Rod Neubert, DVM
2 kg (4 lb) 7 lbs 8 oz/3.42 kg Sandspit, British Columbia 30 August 1984 Gordon Prentice
4 kg (8 lb) 11 lbs 8 oz/5.21 kg Karluk River, Alaska 13 July 1984 Rod Neubert, DVM
6 kg (12 lb) 12 lbs 9 oz/5.69 kg Moose & Kenai rivers, Alaska 17 August 1974 Steven Alan Lee
8 kg (16 lb) 10 lbs 2 oz/4.60 kg Snohomish River, Washington 13 September 1985 F. John Erickson
10 kg (20 lb) 7 lbs 13 oz/3.56 kg Kenai River, Alaska 12 August 1984 Jeff Trom
15 kg (30 lb) 6 lbs 5 oz/2.86 kg Kenai River, Alaska 5 August 1984 Fred Pentt
Fly Rod - Tippet Class
1 kg (2 lb) 10 lbs/4.53 kg Karluk River, Alaska 13 July 1984 Rod Neubert, D.V.M.
2 kg (4 lb) 11 lbs 8 oz/5.21 kg Karluk River, Alaska 10 July 1984 Rod Neubert, D.V.M.
4 kg (8 lb) 3 lbs 14 oz/1.75 kg Kanektok River, Alaska 8 July 1982 Joe Ganim
6 kg (12 lb) 6 lbs 13 oz/3.11 kg Salmon Creek, Alaska 31 July 1985 Bob Garfield
8 kg (16 lb) 5 lbs 10 oz/2.57 kg Buskin River, Alaska 28 July 1986 Terry Stockman

SALMON: sockeye (*Oncorhynchus nerka*) 12 lbs 8 oz/5.66 kg Situk River, Alaska 23 June 1983 Mike Boswell
Line Class
1 kg (2 lb) 10 lbs/4.53 kg Russian River, Alaska 15 August 1985 Glenn Quick
2 kg (4 lb) 10 lbs 15 oz/4.96 kg Russian River, Alaska 14 August 1984 Martin Vanderploeg
4 kg (8 lb) 12 lbs/5.44 kg Kenai River, Alaska 23 July 1984 Richard G. Kincaid
6 kg (12 lb) 11 lbs 3 oz/5.07 kg Kenai River, Alaska 8 August 1982 Warren C. Hoflich
8 kg (16 lb) 12 lbs 8 oz/5.66 kg Situk River, Alaska 23 June 1983 Mike Boswell
10 kg (20 lb) 12 lbs 2 oz/5.50 kg Kenai River, Alaska 29 August 1986 Galen (Skip) Perry
15 kg (30 lb) 12 lbs/5.44 kg Kenai River, Alaska 17 August 1984 Galen M. Perry
Fly Rod - Tippet Class
1 kg (2 lb) 9 lbs 1 oz/4.11 kg Newhalen River,

Alaska 4 July 1985 Bruce Gernon
2 kg (4 lb) 10 lbs 15 oz/4.97 kg Kenai River, Alaska 30 August 1986 Roberta J. Knapp
4 kg (8 lb) 10 lbs 3 oz/4.62 kg Kanektok River, Alaska 6 July 1984 Jim Teeny
6 kg (12 lb) 10 lbs 7 oz/4.73 kg Brooks River, Alaska 22 August 1983 Jim Teeny
8 kg (16 lb) 10 lbs 3 oz/4.62 kg Kanektok River, Alaska 5 July 1986 Walker L. Hughes

SHAD: American (*Alosa sapidissima*) 1 lbs 4 oz/ 5.10 kg Connecticut River, Massachusetts 19 May 1986 Bob Thibodo
Line Class
1 kg (2 lb) 7 lbs 6 oz/3.34 kg Delaware River, Pennsylvania 10 May 1984 Ronald Yates
2 kg (4 lb) 8 lbs 14 oz/4.02 kg Delaware River, New Jersey 29 April 1984 André Moirano
4 kg (8 lb) 11 lbs 1 oz/5.01 kg Delaware River, New Jersey 5 May 1984 Charles J. Mower
6 kg (12 lb) 11 lbs 4 oz/5.10 kg Connecticut River, Massachusetts 19 May 1986 Bob Thibodo
Fly Rod - Tippet Class
1 kg (2 lb) 7 lbs 4 oz/3.28 kg Feather River, California 30 June 1983 Rod Neubert, D.V.M.
2 kg (4 lb) 5 lbs 9 oz/2.53 kg Delaware River, Pennsylvania 9 May 1986 Dave Wonderlich
4 kg (8 lb) 6 lbs 7 oz/2.92 kg Yuba River, California 30 May 1981 Eugene W. Schweitzer
6 kg (12 lb) 3 lbs 13 oz/1.72 kg Indianhead River, Massachusetts 20 May 1986 David Pickering
8 kg (16 lb) 5 lbs/2.26 kg Columbia River, Washington 14 June 1986 William J. Harris

SHEEFISH: (*Stenodus leucichthys*) 53 lbs/ 24.04 kg Pah River, Alaska 20 August 1986 Lawrence E. Hudnall
Line Class
1 kg (2 lb) 24 lbs/10.88 kg Pah River, Alaska 19 August 1986 Lawrence E. Hudnall
2 kg (4 lb) 38 lbs 2 oz/17.29 kg Kobuk River, Alaska 12 September 1982 Mark Feldman, M.D.
4 kg (8 lb) 39 lbs/17.69 kg Kobuk River, Alaska 20 August 1986 Daniel J. Hudnall
6 kg (12 lb) 33 lbs 9 oz/15.22 kg Kobuk River, Alaska 29 August 1981 John A. Berg
8 kg (16 lb) 34 lbs/15.42 kg Kobuk River, Alaska 21 August 1986 Lawrence E. Hudnall
10 kg (20 lb) 53 lbs/24.04 kg Pah River, Alaska 20 August 1986 Lawrence E. Hudnall
15 kg (30 lb) 25 lbs/11.33 kg Kobuk River, Alaska 6 June 1986 Michael M. Hamrick
24 kg (50 lb) 25 lbs/11.33 kg Kobuk River, Alaska 19 August 1986 Daniel J. Hudnall
Fly Rod - Tippet Class
1 kg (2 lb) 16 lbs 8 oz/7.48 kg Hoholitna River, Alaska 23 June 1982 Edward J. Cramer
2 kg (4 lb) 13 lbs/5.89 kg Hoholitna River, Alaska 23 June 1984 Elmer M. Rusten
4 kg (8 lb) 11 lbs/4.98 kg Kobuk River, Alaska 28 August 1981 George Gehrke
6 kg (12 lb) 18 lbs/8.16 kg Pah River, Alaska 19 August 1986 Lawrence E. Hudnall
8 kg (16 lb) 17 lbs 9 oz/7.96 kg Kobuk River, Alaska 28 August 1981 Jim Teeny

SUNFISH: green (*Lepomis cyanellus*) 2 lbs 2 oz/0.96 kg Stockton Lake, Missouri 18 June 1971 Paul M. Dilley
All classes are VACANT

SUNFISH: longear (*Lepomis megalotis*) 1 lb 12 oz/0.79 kg Elephant Butte Lake, New Mexico 9 May 1985 Patricia Stout

SUNFISH: pumpkinseed (*Lepomis gibbosus*) 1

lb 6 oz/0.63 kg Mexico, New York 27 April 1985 Heather Ann Finch

SUNFISH: redbreast (*Lepomis auritus*) 1 lb 12 oz/ 0.79 kg Suwannee River, Florida 29 May 1984 Alvin Buchanan
Line Class
1 kg (2 lb) 1 lb 1 oz/0.48 kg Suwanee River, Florida 29 June 1986 Winston Baker
2 kg (4 lb) 1 lb 4 oz/0.56 kg Suwanee River, Florida 4 November 1984 Winston Baker
4 kg (8 lb) 1 lb 12 oz/0.79 kg Suwanee River, Florida 29 May 1984 Alvin Buchanan
6 kg (12 lb) 1 lb 2 oz/0.51 kg Suwanee River, Florida 23 July 1986 Bernard L. Schultz
Fly Rod - Tippet Class
All fly rod classes are VACANT

SUNFISH: redear (*Lepomis microlophus*) 4 lbs 13 oz/ 2.20 kg Merritt's Mill Pond, Florida 13 March 1986 Joey M. Floyd
Line Class
1 kg (2 lb) 2 lbs 2 oz/0.97 kg Alamance Lake, North Carolina 23 September 1984 Roy E. Jones
2 kg (4 lb) 2 lbs 12 oz/1.26 kg Conyer's, Georgia 22 June 1979 Loy P. Croker
4 kg (8 lb) 4 lbs 10 oz/2.09 kg Merritt's Mill Pond, Florida 23 May 1985 C.L. Windham
6 kg (12 lb) 4 lbs 13 oz/2.20 kg Merritt's Mill Pond, Florida 13 March 1986 Joey M. Floyd
Fly Rod - Tippet Class
1 kg (2 lb) 1 lb 4 oz/0.58 kg Merritt's Mill Pond, Florida 30 September 1986 Jerry Hill
2 kg (4 lb) 1 lb 14 oz/0.85 kg St. Johns River, Florida 1 November 1982 Marie Gardner
All other fly rod classes are VACANT

TROUT: brook (*Salvelinus fontinalis*) 14 lbs 8 oz/6.57 kg Nipigon River, Ontario July 1916 Dr. W.J. Cook
Line Class
1 kg (2 lb) 7 lbs 8 oz/3.40 kg Misstassini River, Quebec 1 September 1982 Bill Atwood
2 kg (4 lb) 8 lbs 4 oz/3.74 kg Minipi River, Labrador 9 August 1986 Parrie F. Willette
4 kg (8 lb) 6 lbs 8 oz/2.94 kg Lake Michigan, Wisconsin 30 June 1986 William H. Vance
6 kg (12 lb) 6 lbs 4 oz/2.83 kg Lake Michigan, Wisconsin 26 June 1985 Sharon E. Keas
8 kg (16 lb) 5 lbs 14 oz/2.66 kg Bee Lake, Ontario 14 August 1983 Stanley Schroeder
10 kg (20 lb) 4 lbs 3 oz/1.92 kg Ashuanipi River, Labrador 3 July 1986 Raymond Carignan
Fly Rod - Tippet Class
1 kg (2 lb) 8 lbs 4 oz/3.74 kg Minonipi River, Labrador 8 July 1980 Harvey S. Smith
2 kg (4 lb) 9 lbs/4.08 kg Little Airy Lake, Labrador 18 July 1981 Harvey S. Smith
4 kg (8 lb) 10 lbs 7 oz/4.73 kg Broadback River, Quebec 5 September 1982 James F. McGarry
6 kg (12 lb) Broadback River, Quebec 2 September 1986 Peter M. Baskin
8 kg (16 lb) 6 lbs 8 oz/2.94 kg Minipi River, Labrador 20 August 1986 Harry Robertson III

TROUT: brown (*Salmo trutta*) 35 lbs 5 oz/16.30 kg Nahuel Huapi, Argentina 16 December 1952 Eugenio Cavaglia
Line Class
1 kg (2 lb) 14 lbs 6 oz/6.54 kg White River, Arkansas 1 February 1986 Anthony J. Salamon
2 kg (4 lb) 27 lbs 9 oz/12.50 kg White River, Arkansas 27 June 1981 Stanford D. Shanker
4 kg (8 lb) 33 lbs 8 oz/15.19 kg White River, Arkansas 19 March 1977 Leon L. Wagoner
6 kg (12 lb) 34 lbs 6 oz/15.59 kg Bar Lake,

Michigan 16 May 1984 Robert Henderson
8 kg (16 lb) 21 lbs 5 oz/9.68 kg Lake Michigan, Wisconsin 7 August 1982 Bert Coltman
10 kg (20 lb) 24 lbs 12 oz/11.22 kg Lake Michigan, Michigan 1 July 1984 Gayle Hoenke
15 kg (30 lb) 17 lbs 10 oz/8.00 kg Stockholm Stream, Sweden 3 November 1983 Magnus Herou
24 kg (50 lb) 14 lbs 4 oz/6.46 kg Lake Ontario, New York 29 April 1986 Paul Loquasto

Fly Rod - Tippet Class
1 kg (2 lb) 10 lbs 9 oz/4.80 kg Tongariro River, New Zealand 6 July 1986 Tuhi Y. Thompson
2 kg (4 lb) 11 lbs 9 oz/5.26 kg Tongariro River, New Zealand 23 May 1985 Louie Denolfo
4 kg (8 lb) 27 lbs 3 oz/12.33 kg Flaming Gorge Reservoir, Utah 13 April 1978 Joe Butler
6 kg (12 lb) 12 lbs/5.44 kg Lake Michigan, Wisconsin 24 November 1984 Allan L. Gens
8 kg (16 lb) 4 lbs 11 oz/2.12 kg Ryan Creek, Wisconsin 8 June 1986 Martin Frame

TROUT: cutthroat (*Salmo clarki*) 41 lbs/18.59 kg Pyramid Lake, Nevada December 1925 John Skimmerhorn
Line Class
1 kg (2 lb) 9 lbs 14 oz/4.50 kg Pyramid Lake, Nevada 21 July 1984 Ray Johnson
2 kg (4 lb) 10 lbs 14 oz/4.95 kg Pyramid Lake, Nevada 21 July 1984 Ray Johnson
4 kg (8 lb) 13 lbs 8 oz/6.12 kg Pyramid Lake, Nevada 2 February 1986 Jose Silva
6 kg (12 lb) 11 lbs 12 oz/5.32 kg Pyramid Lake, Nevada 8 November 1985 John A. Gorzelny
8 kg (16 lb) 11 lbs 12 oz/5.32 kg Pyramid Lake, Nevada 16 February 1986 Robert C. Brunner
10 kg (20 lb) 11 lbs 6 oz/5.16 kg Pyramid Lake, Nevada 30 July 1984 Ray Johnson

Fly Rod - Tippet Class
1 kg (2 lb) 2 lbs 13 oz/1.27 kg Clearwater lake, Montana 17 August 1981 Burton R. Leed
2 kg (4 lb) 4 lbs 7 oz/2.01 kg S. Platte River, Colorado 18 April 1986 John W. Lueckel
4 kg (8 lb) 14 lbs 1 oz/6.37 kg Pyramid Lake, Nevada 4 April 1982 Donald R. Williamson
All other fly rod classes are VACANT

TROUT: golden (*Salmo aguabonita*) 11 lbs/4.98 kg Cooks Lake, Wyoming 5 August 1948 Chas. S. Reed
Line Class
1 kg (2 lb) 2 lbs 2 oz/0.96 kg Bridger Wilderness, Wyoming 6 August 1985 Burton R. Leed
2 kg (4 lb) 1 lb 6 oz/0.62 kg Wind River Range, Wyoming 12 July 1986 Donald J. Dinkel
4 kg (8 lb) 2 lbs/0.92 kg Popo Agie Wilderness, Wyoming 11 July 1986 Dan Thurmond
6 kg (12 lb) 2 lbs 11 oz/1.21 kg Thumb Lake, Wyoming 12 July 1986 Thomas L. Pierce
A remarkable coincidence—three freshwater records set on the same species in the same state in a 24-hour period.
Fly Rod - Tippet Class
All fly rod classes are VACANT

TROUT: lake (*Salvelinus namaycush*) 65 lbs/29.48 kg Great Bear Lake, NWT 8 August 1970 Larry Daunis
Line Class
1 kg (2 lb) 28 lbs 5 oz/12.84 kg Flaming Gorge Reservoir, Utah 31 October 1984 Ray Johnson

2 kg (4 lb) 31 lbs 8 oz/14.28 kg Flaming Gorge Reservoir, Utah 5 November 1984 Ray Johnson
4 kg (8 lb) 38 lbs/17.23 kg Great Bear Lake, Northwest Territories 25 July 1984 Hugh S. Dougan
6 kg (12 lb) 50 lbs 8 oz/22.90 kg Great Bear Lake, Northwest Territories 22 August 1984 Marco J. Zonni
8 kg (16 lb) 53 lbs 4 oz/24.15 kg Great Bear Lake, Northwest Territories 16 July 1986 Richard J. Simourd
10 kg (20 lb) 63 lbs 9 oz/28.83 kg Great Bear Lake, Northwest Territories 31 July 1986 Mike Kroening
15 kg (30 lb) 60 lbs 12 oz/27.55 kg Great Bear Lake, Northwest Territories 26 August 1985 Barbara Goforth
24 kg (50 lb) 50 lbs/22.67 kg Jackson Lake, Wyoming 8 July 1983 Mrs. Doris Budge
37 kg (80 lb) 34 lbs 1 oz/15.45 kg Flaming Gorge Reservoir, Utah 17 November 1984 Ray Johnson
If ever there were a record that seems easy to knock off, consider the 80-lb freshwater class. An even moderately determined effort by an angler visiting Great Bear Lake would likely result in a new entry in the books. Keep it in mind, next time you're in the Territories.

Fly Rod - Tippet Class
1 kg (2 lb) 13 lbs 8 oz/6.12 kg Wellesley Lake, Yukon Territory 12 August 1986 T. Jack Beeler
2 kg (4 lb) 17 lbs 8 oz/7.93 kg Granby Dam, Colorado 18 September 1983 Larry D. Sneith
4 kg (8 lb) 20 lbs 10 oz/9.35 kg Granby Dam, Colorado 18 September 1983 Larry D. Sneith
6 kg (12 lb) 17 lbs 7 oz/7.90 kg Granby Dam, Colorado 18 September 1983 Ken Berkenhotter
8 kg (16 lb) 9 lbs/4.08 kg Selby River, Alaska 16 August 1986 Lawrence E.

TROUT: rainbow (*Salmo gairdneri*) 42 lbs 2 oz/19.10 kg Bell Island, Alaska 22 June 1970 David R. White
Line Class
1 kg (2 lb) 18 lbs 4 oz/8.27 kg Cowlitz River, Washington 4 July 1981 Larry Johnson
2 kg (4 lb) 23 lbs 12 oz/10.77 kg Bowmanville Creek, Ontario 28 April 1984 Brett Elliott
4 kg (8 lb) 26 lbs 9 oz/12.04 kg Lake Pend Oreille, Idaho 18 October 1982 Robert E. Pugh
6 kg (12 lb) 29 lbs 1 oz/13.18 kg Skeena River, British Columbia 12 November 1976 Day B. Karr
8 kg (16 lb) 30 lbs 9 oz/13.86 kg Lake Pend Oreille, Idaho 6 May 1980 Jack Wilkinson
10 kg (20 lb) 31 lbs 5 oz/14.20 kg Lake Pend Oreille, Idaho 19 November 1983 Gilbert Norlen
15 kg (30 lb) 30 lbs 5 oz/13.74 kg Thompson River, British Columbia 5 November 1984 Buzz Ramsey
24 kg (50 lb) 18 lbs 15 oz/8.58 kg Portage, Indiana 23 July 1986 Jack A. Davis

Fly Rod - Tippet Class
1 kg (2 lb) 16 lbs 8 oz/7.48 kg Salmon River, New York 22 February 1982 Francis J. Verdoliva, Jr.
2 kg (4 lb) 19 lbs 13 oz/9.00 kg Little Calumet River, Indiana 6 September 1982 Roger D. Enyeart
4 kg (8 lb) 24 lbs 8 oz/11.11 kg Sustut River, British Columbia 22 September 1982 Bruce Gernon
6 kg (12 lb) 22 lbs 8 oz/10.20 kg Rogue River, Michigan 1 April 1981 Glen D. Peoples

8 kg (16 lb) 28 lbs/12.70 kg Skeena River, British Columbia 20 October 1985 Chuck Stephens

WALLEYE: (*Stizostedion vitreum vitreum*) 25 lbs/11.34 kg Old Hickory Lake, Tennessee 1 April 1960 Mabry Harper
Line Class
1 kg (2 lb) 10 lbs 6 oz/4.70 kg Branched Oak Lake, Nebraska 18 April 1984 Thomas G. Bitting
2 kg (4 lb) 18 lbs 4 oz/8.27 kg Little Red River, Arkansas 14 March 1983 Mark S. Wallace
4 kg (8 lb) 19 lbs 5 oz/8.75 kg Greers Ferry Lake, Arkansas 2 March 1982 Erma W. Windorff
6 kg (12 lb) 22 lbs 11 oz/10.29 kg Greers Ferry Lake, Arkansas 14 March 1982 Al Nelson
8 kg (16 lb) 18 lbs 4 oz/8.27 kg Greers Ferry Lake, Arkansas 12 January 1982 Howard L. Brierly
10 kg (20 lb) 15 lbs 2 oz/6.86 kg Columbia River, Oregon 16 July 1984 Dan Nelson

Fly Rod - Tippet Class
1 kg (2 lb) 1 lb 14 oz/0.85 kg Strammond Lake, Quebec 10 June 1986 Dave Wonderlich
2 kg (4 lb) 5 lbs 12 oz/2.60 kg Mistassini, Quebec 19 June 1983 Bill Atwood
4 kg (8 lb) 8 lbs 10 oz/3.91 kg Humboldt River, Nevada 6 June 1984 Paul E. Bezayiff
6 kg (12 lb) 1 lb 5 oz/0.59 kg Strammond Lake, Quebec 10 June 1986 Thomas Heffernan
8 kg (16 lb) 5 lbs 2 oz/2.32 kg Lake Erie, Ohio 22 September 1985 Ben Doepel

Index

Numbers in italics indicate illustrations

Barracuda, 99-101
Bass, 11-20. *See also* Channel bass, striped bass
    crappie, 18
    largemouth, 11, 14, *15, 16, 17, 19*
    smallmouth, *12-13*, 18, *20*
    white, 144, *146-147*
    whiterock, 144
Billfish, 102-111. *See also* Marlin, Sailfish, Swordfish
    equipment for, 111
Billfish Foundation, The, 109
Bluefish, 97, 112-113, 119, 138
    tackle for, 112-113
Bluegill, 30-33. *See also* Sunfish
    bait for, 30-33
Bonefish, 114-115, *116-117*, 118, 125, 136
    stalking, 114-115
Bonito, 118-119
    tackle for, 118-119
Boston pollock. *See* Bluefish
Braddick, Donnie, 137
Canso Strait, 150
Catfish, 21-27
    bait for, 22-23
    blue, 21, *26-27*
    bullhead, *21*
    channel, 21-22, *24-25*
    flathead, 22
    hornpout, *21*, 23
    spotted, *22-23*
    white, 23
Channel bass, 97, 128, *130*
Charr, 85, 93. *See also* Trout
Ciampi, Elgin, 18
Columbia River, 57
Connecticut River, 66
    Enfield Dan, 66
Crappie, 18, *31*
Delaware River, 66
Dolly Varden. *See* Trout, Dolly Varden
Dolphin, 120, *121, 122-123*
Grayling, 28-29, 58, 93
Green, Seth, 66
Hornpout. *See* Catfish, bullhead
Hudson River, 66
International Game Fish Association (IGFA), 28, 36, 56, 57, 101, 106, 148, 150
Jackfish, 38
Kenai River, 57
Kobuk River, 68

Lake Maracaibo, 148
Lake Ponchartrain, 142
Largemouth bass, 11, 14, *15, 16, 17, 19*
Long Island Sound, 97
Mahi-mahi. *See* Dolphin
Marlin, 102-106, 109, 111
    black, 102, 106, *108-109*
    blue, *103, 104-105*, 106
    striped, 106, 107
    tackle for, 102
    white, 102-106
Minipi River, 82
Mudcats. *See* Catfish, flathead
Mundus, Frank, 137
Muskellunge, *39, 42, 43*
    tiger, 42
National Marine Fisheries Service, 106
Panfish, 30-35
Perch, 36-37
    walleye, 36, *37*
    Yellow, 36-37
Permit, *124*, 125, *126-127*
Pickerel, *39*, 41
Pikes, 38-45, 99
    muskellunge, *39, 42, 43*, 99
    northern, 38-41, *44-45*, 58
    pickerel, *39*, 41
    shooting, 41-42
    tackle for, 41
Pompano, 125
Red drum. *See* Redfish
Redfish, 128, *129, 130, 131*
Rockfish, 144
Rogue River, 61
Sailfish, 98, 107, *108, 110-111*
Salmon, 28
    Atlantic, 46, *50-51, 52-54*, 66
    chinook, 57
    chum, *56*, 57-58
    coho, 48-49, 58-61
    dog, *56*, 57-58
    fingerlings, 52-54
    gruse, *53*
    humpback, 57, *59*
    king, 57, *64-65*
    landlocked, 55-56, *61*
    parr, 54
    red, 58, *62-63*
    silver, 60-61
    sockeye, *47*, 58, *62-63*
    spawning of, 46-52
Saltwater fish, 97-98

Sea trout, 156, *157*, 158
  spotted, *157*, 158
Shad, 66-67
  hickory, *66, 67*
Sheefish, 68-69
  Alaskan, *69*
Sharks, 99, 106, 132
  blacktip, *132-133*, 136
  blue, 137
  cautions, 132-136
  great white, 137
  lemon, *136*
  mako, 137
  tackle for, 137
  tiger, *134-135*
Shellcracker, *See* Sunfish
Smallmouth bass, *12-13*, 18, 20
Snook, 138, *139, 140-141*
  tackle for, 138
St. Lawrence River, 142
Steelhead, *60*, 61, *72*
Striped bass, 98, 142-144, *145*
  hybrids of, 144
  tackle for, 142
Sunfish, 30-35
  bluegill, 30-33, *34-35*
  crappie, *32*
  green, 33
  long-eared, *32*, 33
  pumpkinseed, 33
  redbreast, 33
  redear, 33
  spotted, 33
Sunshine bass, 144

Swordfish, 106-109, 111
Tarpon, 68, 97, 98, 101, 114, 125, 138, 148-149
  tackle for, 148-149
Thompson River, 61
Trout, 58, 70. *See also* Steelhead
  Arctic charr, 93
  brook, 78-82, *83*
  brown, 70-76, *93*, 97
  Canadian red, *77*
  cutthroat, 82, *88-89, 90-91*
  Dolly Varden, 28, 58, 85, *86-87*, 93
  golden, 82-85
  lake, *84*, 85, *92*
  leopard rainbow, 74, 77
  rainbow, 61, *75*, 76-77, *92, 94*
  sunapee, *72*
  Tahoe, *92*
Tunas, 118, 150-155
  albacore, 150
  allison, 150
  baits for, 155
  bigeye, 154
  blackfin, 150, *151*
  bluefin, 97, 106, 150, *152-153*, 154-155
  little tunny, 150
  skipjack, 150
  tunny, 150
  yellowfin, 150-154, *155*
Umpqua River, 61
Walleye pike, 36, *37*
Weakfish, 156, *157*, 158
White bass, 144, *146-147*
Whiterock bass, 144
Wulff, Lee, 54-55